In the Shadow of Empires

Empires

The historic Vlad Dracula, the events he shaped and the events that shaped him.

Sir Jens

First Break
Publishing

Published by First Break Publishing

ISBN: 978-0-9576-4720-6

This book is also available as an eBook. For details please visit
www.firstbreakpublishing.com or www.sirjens.com.

DEDICATION

This book is for my mother who never answered a question without first asking 'did you look it up in the encyclopedia?'

CONTENTS

FOREWORD

In the summer of 2002, I accepted a job in Transylvania, more precisely in Cluj-Napoca. Having spent a good part of my youth as an officer in an army that saw Eastern Europe as the defined enemy, my hands-on experience with this part of the World was very limited.

Thus, I arrived with few assumptions or expectations and concentrated on matters practical. My sub-conscience, however, had a different view, but such had yet to come to the fore.

As a history buff with an inquisitive nature, it did not take long to find the National Museum of Transylvania tucked away in a dusty side street in the old part of the town, and on a cold and dark December day, I went in.

The museum was open, in a kind of Romanian fashion, which means that all the lights were off and the main entry had been covered by an old blanket to maintain what little heat could be preserved in lieu of a broken central heating system. Not deterred I bought my twenty-five Eurocents ticket and got stuck in. I was followed around by a custodian, whom would go ahead of me, turn the lights on in the next room and then drift back behind me to turn the lights off in the room I had just left. All the explanatory texts were in Romanian, which at the time meant little to me, but as that is exactly the level of commercialism and mass tourism that suits me best I was enjoying myself no end.

Somewhere halfway through the museum, where we had got to the late middle ages, there was a discreet display of pictures of various kings and princes of the surrounding area, and there, tucked in between other former dignitaries, was a small black and white picture with an explanatory text that said 'Vlad Dracula III – Voivode'.

This was the point where my sub-conscience woke up, and by the time I left the museum a question had started to formulate in a more immediate part of my brain; 'where is Dracula?'

I mean I was in the middle of Transylvania, and there should be Dracula everywhere, shouldn't there? Mugs, restaurants, ball-pens and such other trinkets, perhaps a dedicated museum and at least some kind of signpost pointing to Dracula's castle. But no, there was nothing, apart from that dusty picture among others similar, in a non-descript room inside an equally non-descript museum in a place that few had ever heard of.

Something was wrong, so with the question now at the forefront of my mind I started asking the locals. The best answer I could get, over and above a shake of the shoulders, was 'well, he is not from Transylvania'.

Whoa, hold on! Everybody knows that Dracula is from Transylvania, how stupid do these people think I am? Then when I actually started to nose around on the subject, I found out that they were technically right, and that Dracula was really from Wallachia, the part of modern day Romania south of the Carpathians. But how could that be? Why did

I, like probably ninety-nine % of the world's population think that Dracula was from Transylvania?

I was now intrigued, and not less so when one of the locals, trying to at least give me something to work on, told me that Dracula is a popular Romanian folk hero, someone of whom the Romanians think back to as an icon of law and order, and that Romanian children will learn in school the (strongly nationalistic) 'Scrisoarea a iii a' poem by poet laureate Mihai Eminescu, which ends:

> 'O, leave in the old chronicles our forefathers to rest;
> For they would gaze upon you with irony at best.
> Rise once more, o Tepes ! Take and divide these men
> As lunatics and rogues in two big tribes, and then
> In mighty, twin infirmaries by force both tribes intern,
> And with a single faggot prison and madhouse burn.'

The 'Tepes' referred to is of course Vlad Dracula, 'Tepes' or 'the Impaler' being one of the names by which Vlad Dracula has come to be known over time.

As helpful as that was intended to be, this just left me with yet another question; 'is this guy a hero or a villain?' Surely he can't be both a bloodthirsty tyrant and a national icon of law and order at the same time? Actually he can, and indeed he is.

I now started to throw myself at every available source of information about Vlad Dracula, and I soon figured a few things out.

Firstly, if I wanted my questions answered I had to completely ignore the vampire. As much as Bram Stoker's choice of villain has participated to make Dracula a household name, this is all nineteenth century fiction written by a talented storywriter who never actually set foot in Transylvania, but who late in the process of finishing his vampire novel stumbled across Dracula and Transylvania, and liked the name and the place so much that he literally wrote it into an otherwise nearly finished story.

Secondly, having left the vampire behind, most of the available historic literature is written by academics. That is useful for reference, source criticism etc. but it is almost impossible to read (being as full of notes, footnotes and references as there is text), and it most certainly does not compel a general audience to try to follow an intriguing story to the end.

Thirdly, to understand and explain Vlad Dracula you need to understand and explain his times and the other people who had a direct impact on him and his world. The Story of Vlad thus becomes a mix of micro-views when there are historical facts about Vlad himself to build on and macro-views where Vlad's story can best be told by looking at his surrounding world. Through this a picture also emerges of four heroes, so alike and yet so different, but we shall save that part for later.

Last, someone should really write this story down in a manner that is accessible, perhaps even interesting and this is my attempt at it.

Because of the mix of fiction, superstition and academia that makes up the available sources on Vlad Dracula, the picture that emerges when you start to take it all apart and bring it back together again is confusing, often conflicting and most certainly incomplete.

Original sources are rare, and when available mostly written in languages I don't master (the official language that was used for written records in fifteenth century Wallachia was for example Church Slavic). I therefore have to rely on other people's translations, but where possible I have compiled my own translation from as many of those as possible.

Similarly, fifteenth century written records were as often as not subject to incestuous amplification, i.e. written to conform to an opinion, or bias, already predominant with the intended reader. It was for example not a route to a long life for an Ottoman chronicler to write something negative about the sultan, so any Ottoman setbacks would be either completely ignored or whitewashed in the records.

I often remind myself of the scientists in Jurassic Park, who extract dinosaur DNA from ancient amber, but come up with incomplete DNA strands. Even after combining several incomplete strands they still do not have a complete strand and to solve that problem they use frog DNA to fill in the blanks, and I have had to do the same.

I am not an academic, and this book is not an academic thesis. It is an attempt to tell a compelling story that is true to the extent such truth can be found and which is filled in by the best fitting frog DNA where no other option is available. It is thus probably subject to errors and omissions, and some may choose to focus on those, but I hope it makes the man, Vlad Dracula, a little bit more available to a broader audience.

This is the book I would have liked to pick up when I left the National Museum of Transylvania in December 2002.

Sir Jens

Sir Jens

MAPS

Balkans, Geographical Map, c. 1460

Balkans, Political Map, c. 1460

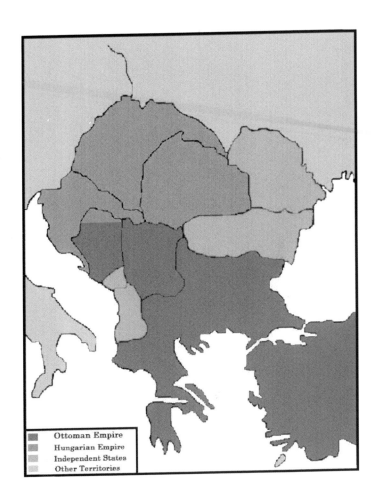

Ottoman Empire
Hungarian Empire
Independent States
Other Territories

Sir Jens

CHAPTER 1
IN THE SHADOW OF EMPIRES

Sir Jens

Fault lines

When on a cold winter's day in 1431 a baby boy was born in the Transylvanian town of Sighisoara, no one would have known, or even imagined, that this boy would become not only a legend in his own time, evenly vilified and glorified by his contemporaries, but would indeed become an immortal icon for both good and evil.

Born as the third son to a Wallachian nobleman, of royal blood, the likely fate of the newborn baby was that of either relative, but comfortable, obscurity or, more likely, a turbulent and violent life ending in early death, probably by the hands of his own blood-relatives.

The boy was named Vladislav after his father, shortened to Vlad in common use, and as his father had recently taken use of the surname Dracul (the Dragon), Vlad would be given the surname Dracula (of the Dragon).

This of course would become the very name that has reverberated through the centuries since, but before we continue on that journey, we need to set the scene and understand the environment that little Vlad was born into, and which would govern the formation and definition of the man he was to become, and the man others would perceive him to be.

Fifteenth century Balkans was on a juncture of fault lines. Religions met opposing religions, cultures clashed with other cultures, super-powers fought for supremacy, and an undergrowth of political and commercial special-interest groups threw their own logs onto an already blazing fire.

These fault lines were not necessarily new, but at this time they were in a state of constant activity, edges grinding against each other, causing change and upheaval, war and famine, revolt and oppression, lawlessness and disorder.

Such circumstances were shared by all inhabitants of the region, high and low, but whereas commoners could find extended periods of relative peace, typically when active conflicts were currently in different theatres, baby Vlad was unlikely to ever find such peace. The very blood that ran in his veins made him a 'player'; if not through his own doing, then as a suitable pawn in someone else's power game.

And so the story begins with a look at some of the countries, cultures and religions that shaped the raw edges of these fault lines.

The Hungarian Kingdom and Transylvania

The Hungarian Kingdom became a unified Christian state in the early eleventh century and had since emerged as a regional powerhouse. Aggressive expansion into south Eastern Europe had by the early part of the fifteenth century created a Hungarian Empire that effectively stretched in a belt from the Adriatic Sea in the West to the Black Sea in the East, sealing off the northern border of the Balkan Peninsula.

The Christian world that lay beyond the Hungarian Empire was one of division, mistrust and had its own collection of fault lines and conflict.

The powerful nations of England and France were involved in a war with each other that would last more than a hundred years.

The Germans states, nominally united in the Holy Roman Empire, were as disunited as ever and had their main focus on eastwards expansion.

The disparate Spanish and Portuguese kingdoms were busy keeping an eye on each other and the remaining Muslim enclave in Grenada. To the extent they had interests outside their immediate area, they mainly thought like explorers and traders and they were sailing west and south.

Italy was split into rivaling principalities and merchant states, constantly at each other's throats militarily or commercially.

The Papal State had no less than three competing popes until, following the Hungarian King Sigismund's initiative, the Council of Constance managed to bring that back to only one pope, in Rome. Whereas The Pope had resources, it was mainly monetary and he depended on others to do the actual fighting.

Poland was busy trying to push back the advances of the Germans, in particular the Teutonic Knights, and of the Tartars coming up from the Crimean peninsula.

The Russian nation was only slowly forming, having only recently emerged from Mongol domination, and they were yet to become the powerhouse they would later be.

So, really, Hungary was to a large extent on its own when facing the new kid on the block, the Ottoman Empire.

The Hungarians and the Ottomans had fought it out several times, though mainly with the Hungarians in a supportive role to others, unsuccessfully trying to prevent the Ottomans overrunning Bulgaria and Serbia and establishing themselves directly on the southern border of Hungary and Christianity itself.

Since a major defeat to the Ottomans at Nicopolis in 1396, the Hungarians had tried to avoid direct conflict, and put their faith in the Ottoman expansion running out of steam, but that didn't seem to be the case as the Ottomans established themselves solidly in the Balkans by annexation of Bulgaria and de-facto sovereignty of Serbia.

An area annexed by the Hungarians for centuries was Transylvania, the north western part of modern day Romania, separated East and South by the Carpathian Mountains.

The indigenous population of Transylvania was culturally and religiously different from their Hungarian overlords, and thus we have fault lines inside fault lines.

The Hungarians spoke Hungarian or Latin (Latin being the official language of Hungary until 1844), whereas the Transylvanians spoke a language similar to modern day Romanian (which in itself is strongly based on Latin). The Hungarians were Roman Catholics and thus spiritually obedient to Rome, whereas the indigenous Transylvanians were Greek Orthodox and thus spiritually obedient to Constantinople.

In 1241 the Mongol Golden Horde invaded large parts of Hungary including Transylvania and even though they didn't stay for long due to the death of their Khan and an ensuing internal power struggle, this event had a deep impact on the way Transylvania looked at the beginning of the fifteenth Century.

Following the Mongol invasion, the Hungarian king Béla IV blew new life into the emigration policy of foreign (mostly Germanic, and thus commonly referred to as "Saxon") traders and knights that had initially been started by his predecessor King Géza II in the previous century. His offer included substantial tax benefits and a high level of autonomy in exchange for the fortification of a range of Transylvanian towns, better to withstand further invasion attempts. The strategy was successful, in that further Mongol attempts were repelled, and it led to the formation of seven strongly defended "Saxon" towns in Transylvania. Indeed, in the German language, Transylvania is still called Siebenbürgen (Seven Castles).

Each of these Saxon towns paid homage, and taxes, to the Hungarian king, but were in most other aspects run like independent, German speaking, merchant towns, ruled by the professional guilds. Each guild was responsible for the building, maintenance and, in times of unrest, manning of a specific part of the town wall, including one bastion or tower. Some of these walls and bastions can still be seen in Transylvanian towns such as Brasov, Sibiu and Cluj-Napoca.

The Ottoman Empire

Despite the fact that the Islamic Empire, started by Muhammad and expanded for decades after his death, never controlled Anatolia, also known as Asia Minor, the religion of Islam itself had gradually moved north, and by the fourteenth Century all of Anatolia was Islamic.

After the collapse of the Seljuk Turk state and with Mongol influence waning, Anatolia had turned into a patchwork of feudal principalities, or beyliks.

This is not dissimilar to how Western Europe had developed in the centuries since the collapse of the Roman Empire, and there was no central authority, or nation state, to unify these disparate enclaves though over and above being Islamic they also, mainly, shared the Turkish language.

Over time these beyliks challenged each other for power and land and one smallish beylik known as the House of Osman, a name that would gradually become "Ottoman", originating round the city of Bursa, would gradually emerge as the dominant player in Anatolia.

The emerging Ottoman state showed great respect for the populations it took over, granting them extensive religious freedom and autonomy, so most conquered populations soon grew to enjoy a level of peace, stability, law and order that far outdid what had been provided to them previously which inspired an emerging fierce loyalty to the new state.

In the middle part of the fourteenth century, internal rivalry in the Byzantine Empire saw one of the Byzantine contesters to the throne enter into an alliance with the Ottomans across the narrow sea and allowed Ottoman troops to land in Europe in support of his campaign.

The Ottomans never went home, but rather occupied the area around Gallipoli and gradually expanded to occupy what is the modern day European part of Turkey, apart from the area around the Byzantine capital, Constantinople, itself.

In 1365, the Ottoman Bay, Murad I, declared Edirne (formerly known as Adrianople) as the Rumelian (European) capital of the Ottoman state, and in 1383 he declared himself Sultan of what was now becoming an Empire proper.

Through the latter part of the fourteenth century the Ottomans expanded into Bulgaria, Northern Greece and Serbia, thus shaping the fault lines that would come to define the region in the fifteenth century.

The Byzantine Empire

The Byzantine, or Eastern Roman, Empire came into existence in the fourth century when the Roman Empire had grown to such a size that it was effectively split into a Western part, ruled from Rome, and an Eastern Part ruled from the new imperial capital of Constantinople (formerly known as Byzantium).

After the collapse of the Western Roman Empire in the fifth century, the Eastern Roman Empire became their cultural heirs and even though they spoke Greek, and had few remaining ties to Rome, they called themselves "Romans" and the area around Constantinople itself was known as Rumelia.

At the height of its influence The Byzantine Empire dominated large parts of the coastline round The Mediterranean Sea, but gradually the emerging Islamic State pushed the Byzantine Empire back in the southern part of the empire and Seljuk Turks, followed by Mongols and the Anatolian beyliks, pushed Byzantine possessions in Anatolia westwards so by the fourteenth century the Byzantine Empire was really reduced to Rumelia and Greece, both of which areas would fall under Ottoman influence in the latter part of the fourteenth century, leaving the former so proud empire as a scattered selection of small, geographically separated, enclaves.

Though political, and geographical, dominance were waning, Constantinople still played another important role. It was the centre of the Eastern Church, also known as the (Greek) Orthodox Church.

Where the Catholic Church, headed by the Pope in Rome, had long dominated Western Europe, the Orthodox Church, headed by the Patriarch in Constantinople, had a similar strong grip on Eastern Europe.

These two wings of Christianity had long been at each other's throats in matters of theology, rite and language and they had finally officially split into two in 1054, leaving the Christian world with their own fault line long before Islam became a real threat.

Subsequent events to reunite the two churches had been unsuccessful, and a last attempt in 1439 would lead to such resistance and disagreement that it played a direct role in the final fall of Constantinople to the Ottomans in 1453.

Wallachia

Compared to these empires, emerging and waning, Wallachia was a small player and whereas Wallachia really is a footnote in the greater historical picture it was the center point for Vlad Dracula, and thus for our story.

Fifteenth century Wallachia was situated south of the Carpathians, roughly similar to the southern part of modern Romania. The people, like those in Transylvania, were of the Orthodox faith and they spoke Romanian.

Apart from the mountains that make up the northern border to Transylvania, Wallachia is a mainly flat area that is bordered in the south by the Danube, with Bulgaria and Serbia on the other side of the river. In the West it borders onto Hungary and in the East to Moldavia and the Black Sea, though by the fifteenth century the Ottomans had taken possession of the seaside and effectively left the Danube to form also part of the Eastern border.

Wallachia was a principality, ruled by a prince, or "Voivode", elected by a council of noblemen called Boyars. Thus, rather than having a stable system of succession based on primogeniture (succession by the oldest son), succession was determined as a choice between eligible royal heirs. This in itself could be difficult enough, but there were several aggravating circumstances that made the system disastrous.

The eligible candidates for the Wallachian throne were all male royal offspring, defined as any male that himself was sired by a royal male, in or out of wedlock. So over and above the "legitimate" royal offspring, the stock of potentials was widened by what in most other countries would be seen as "bastards" born outside of wedlock.

Over time, two competing royal lines had developed, the Danesti and the Draculesti (though the later name was only adapted after Vlad Dracula's father took the name Dracul) which in itself would have caused enough competition and backstabbing to cause instability.

There were, however, other factors that majorly contributed to complicate the succession question in Wallachia even further, indeed they would cause more trouble than the lack of primogeniture itself, but to understand that we need to look at why Wallachia was there at all.

By all rights, Wallachia should have been annexed by Hungary or the Ottomans as was the fate of other, larger, states in the area. Wallachia, however, was special because of its geographical position.

If Wallachia had been annexed, the competing Hungarian and Ottoman empires would have had a wide direct border. That was not in anyone's interest as such a border would have been high maintenance, demanding high concentrations of troops and providing little warning should one or the other empire attack.

Instead Wallachia essentially acted as a buffer-zone, reducing the need for border troops and providing ample warning should any off the opposing armies start moving.

Having said that, it was of course an advantage for one empire or the other if the ruler of Wallachia would be sympathetic to that particular party, and it would become a normal state of affairs that one or the other empire would (forcefully) replace the current ruler with a ruler of their own choice.

Similarly in the picture were the Saxon cities of Southern Transylvania. To these, Wallachia was a prosperous market, particularly as the Wallachians were farmers rather than craftsmen, so goods produced in the Saxon towns such as Brasov or Sibiu were in high demand in Wallachia.

Of course to trade in another country you needed trading rights and some kind of favorable agreement on customs and taxes so the Saxon cities would have their own interest in having a friendly Voivode and they were not far behind their imperial counterparts in staging their own violent coups.

If, however, the question of Voivode only came up every few decades through natural death of the incumbent ruler, then perhaps the problem could have been contained, but the ruling class of Boyars were more than happy to take payment from anyone who would make an attractive offer, so rather than waiting for the current ruler to die, the Boyars would readily support successive armed revolts and regime changes as long as the price was right.

Thus armed with an ample supply of royal candidates, two mighty empires, powerful semi-autonomous merchant cities and a corrupt class of Boyars, Wallachia was a regular scene of regicide and fratricide, leaving the country in a constant state of unrest, disorder and unlawfulness.

Moldavia

Moldavia was an area roughly the size of Wallachia, east of Transylvania, north-east of Wallachia and bordering Poland to the north and east.

Moldavia, like Wallachia, was a principality, ruled by a Voivode, and with a similar system of succession, but a generally more loyal class of Boyars meant that Moldavia had less rulers and less unrest.

Having said that, Moldavia had its own problems with staying independent, swaying in loyalty between Hungary and Poland over time, but the Ottomans and the Saxon cities intervened less in Moldavia than they did in Wallachia.

Like the indigenous populations of Transylvania and Wallachia, the people of Moldavia were of the Orthodox faith and spoke Romanian, so those three areas effectively defined their own cultural group, roughly similar to modern day Romania, even though they at that time were split into separate states.

Like Wallachia, Moldavia is not really a major player in the bigger picture, but I mention it because it would come to play an important role in the life of Vlad Dracula.

Inheritance

We now have the players defined and we can sum up the scene.

Squeezed in between two mighty competing empires, both representing vastly different cultures and religions, we have a small principality called Wallachia which only exists as an independent state because it is not in the interest of the surrounding empires to have a wide, shared, border.

The people of Wallachia are of the Orthodox faith, and thus different from either of the empires that surround them. They also speak their own language which they, like their religion, share with the peoples of Transylvania and Moldavia.

Wallachia has a system of succession that is complicated by a vast amount of potential candidates and several powerful parties outside the country with an appetite on who the ruler should be. A self-serving and corrupt class of noble Boyars, nominally responsible for choosing the ruler, enable a string of rulers to violently overthrow each other, casting the country into a state of near-permanent disorder and lawlessness.

So when Vlad Dracula is born as yet another prince of the blood, this is his inheritance and though his life could well be eventful as well as short, little however points to immortality and iconic status.

CHAPTER 2
EARLY YEARS

Sir Jens

Vlad Dracul

If it hadn't been for his third son, named Vlad after himself, Vlad Dracul (whom we shall henceforth refer to as "Vlad Senior" to avoid confusion) would have probably never really made it into any history book of note and even though, through circumstance, he has, it is not really to tell his own story.

That is a shame, because he also had an interesting journey, and I will take this opportunity to tell some of it, even though I am as guilty as others for only really doing so because it is the best way of telling what happened during the early part of Vlad Dracula's life.

Vlad Senior's father was Mircea I, called "Cel Batran" (The Elder) by later day historians. He ruled Wallachia from 1386 till his death in 1418 which sets him apart from most subsequent rulers of Wallachia both in terms of the length of his rule and the fact that he died from natural causes.

Mircea had finally shaped the principality of Wallachia, which at the height of his reign included the easternmost region of Dobrogea, and thus direct access to the Black Sea. However, two years after his death, Dobrogea was taken by the Ottomans and Wallachia became landlocked with only indirect access to the sea through the Danube River.

On Mircea's death his son, and co-ruler, Mihai (I) took the throne, but he was soon killed in battle with the Ottomans in 1420. The throne now went to Mircea's nephew Dan (II) supported by Hungary, but he was overthrown by Radu (II), another of Mircea's sons, supported by the Ottomans. He in turn was overthrown by Dan, who was then overthrown by Radu and so forth no less than four times in seven years until Dan killed Radu in 1427.

Dan ruled until he himself was killed in battle with the Ottomans in 1432 and the throne was taken by Alexandru I, yet another of Mircea's sons who held on to it until he died from illness in 1436.

While Hungary and the Ottomans played ping-pong with the Wallachian throne and family turned on family in bloody coups, Vlad Senior had been shipped off and groomed at the Hungarian Court, outside the immediate range of the Wallachian court's intrigues.

It is hard to say exactly why Mircea had sent his son to be brought up at the Hungarian Court rather than stay and take active part in the chaos and mayhem that made up contemporary Wallachian politics. Some say that he was placed as a hostage, a custom we shall return to later, but I personally find it hard to think that King Sigismund of Hungary would find it necessary to take hostages from Mircea of Walachia, given Mircea's clear support of Hungary throughout his rule.

I would like to think that Mircea had realised that the boy was special, intelligent rather than brutal, and that the boy's best chance of survival lay with diplomacy rather than warfare and that he would be far better off being educated in such matters at the Hungarian Court of King Sigismund. Whichever the reasons, Vlad Senior was sent to the Hungarian Court sometime in the 1390s, when he was probably around ten years old.

The three to four decades between the time he arrived at the Hungarian court and the time when he finally takes the throne of Wallachia would have seen plenty of opportunity for him to be educated both in warfare and diplomacy.

Without going into too much detail about Hungary and King Sigismund himself (although it is another interesting story), Hungary in the early decades of the fifteenth century saw plenty of political intrigue and warfare for Vlad Senior to learn the ropes in a very hands-on manner.

Though he would have probably been too young to participate in the ill-fated Battle of Nicopolis in 1396, in which the Ottomans won an all-out victory over a Hungarian-led army, Sigismund was involved in one armed conflict or another at most times. He faced internal revolt, was at war with Bohemia and Poland and conducted a "crusade" to take control of Croatia. In 1412-13 he fought the Venetians in Italy and in the 1420s he fought the Hussite Wars against the "heretic" supporters of Jan Huss. In 1428 he even managed to go on yet another (insignificant) campaign against the Ottomans.

War of course also feeds diplomacy, if nothing else to keep one's other enemies sweet while one fights someone else, and Sigismund's court was thus constantly on diplomatic missions.

It is documented that Vlad Senior was sent as emissary to the Byzantine Court in Constantinople on one such occasion, as well as he is known to have performed diplomatic negotiations in Poland. There is no record of Vlad Senior actively participating in any of the armed conflict, but it is a reasonable assumption to make that he would have as part of his education as a prince and knight.

An interesting footnote is that the (Greek) record of Vlad Senior's appearance as a diplomat in Constantinople refers to him as 'one of the many bastard sons of Mircea', from which we learn that he is likely to be the offspring of one of Mircea's mistresses rather than his wife. As already covered, that was not a problem in Wallachia, but obviously still caused some offence abroad.

Along the way Sigismund formed the "Order of the Dragon", a (catholic) noble order with the declared purpose of defending the faith. One of the people who were later invited to join the order was Vlad Senior, who following his investiture took the name "Dracul" (Dragon) for his surname and thus gave name to the bloodline of the "Draculesti". An interesting detail is that the word "dracul" in modern day Romanian means "devil" (a dragon being "balaur"), which has given the modern day vampire hunters plenty to chew on, as in modern Romanian the meaning of Dracula is "of the devil", but in the fifteenth century it meant "of the dragon".

Furthermore, the fact that he was invested in the Order of The Dragon tells us something, namely that he must have (at least nominally) converted from his native Orthodox faith to Catholicism as only Catholics were allowed in the order. Though not documented, it is likely that he would have converted back to the Orthodox faith on his later accession to the Wallachian throne.

Sometime around 1430, around the same time Vlad Senior is invested in The Order of the Dragon, he is also appointed Governor of Transylvania, and moves with his family to the (Saxon) town of Sighisoara in central Transylvania. He already has at least one son, Mircea, and Vlad Dracula is, as we have already covered, born in Sighisoara in 1431.

When Vlad Senior's brother Alexandru, the current Voivode of Wallachia, dies in 1436, King Sigismund orders Vlad Senior to form an army and take the vacant throne. Vlad Senior doesn't hesitate but marches on the Wallachian capital of Targoviste with all possible haste. He meets no resistance, and the Boyars quickly confirm him as Voivode. It can safely be assumed that his family, including the now approximately five years old Vlad Dracula, is moved to the palace in Targoviste and there effectively ends Vlad Dracula's direct link with Transylvania.

Vlad Senior now performs the first action that shows that he is smarter than most of his predecessors and that he has probably studied history in order to learn of other's successes and mistakes.

To secure stability in the, highly probably, case that he should be killed, he appoints his (teenage) son Mircea as co-regent. This way he effectively makes Mircea his given successor, a trick he had learnt from his father (Mircea Cel Batran) who successfully did exactly the same thing to secure his son Mihai the throne on his death.

Vlad Senior thus sits on the throne of Wallachia, with a somewhat secured succession plan and the support of the mighty Hungarian Empire, but his strong position doesn't last long. In December 1437 King Sigismund dies and his death throws Hungary into a weakened state of in-fighting and intrigue, leading also to a peasant revolt in Transylvania.

With his supporter gone, Vlad Senior has no power to resist when the Ottoman Sultan, Murad II, proposes a raid into Transylvania in 1438, a raid in which Vlad Senior is known to have taken active part despite his obligations as a member of the Order of the Dragon. In reality he would have had a choice between joining the Ottomans or have the Ottomans loot their way through Wallachia on their way to Transylvania, and he displays a choice very much dictated by realpolitik (real politics) and an appreciation of the situation rather than the kind of brave loyalties that would commonly get people killed.

As the Hungarian Empire reforms, under the nominal sovereignty of the infant-king Ladislav Posthumous, a new powerful personality enters the stage, namely Janos Hunyadi, also known as the White Knight, a self-made warrior who had been knighted by Sigismund in 1409, and who was appointed Governor of Transylvania in (or around) 1439. Janos Hunyadi would become an important influence on Vlad Dracula's life, so we shall meet him again later.

Vlad Senior now deployed all his diplomatic skills, trying to keep on friendly terms with both the Ottomans and the Hungarians (not least the increasingly powerful Janos Hunyadi), and he was reasonably successful for a few years.

In 1443 the stalemate ends. Sultan Murad calls Vlad Senior to the Ottoman Court in Edirne (knows as "The Divine Porte") in order to establish his exact loyalties. With him he has his two sons Vlad and (the two years younger) Radu. A contemporary chronicle says that Vlad Senior lied about the whereabouts of his oldest son (and co-regent) Mircea, declaring him dead. This indicates that Vlad Senior once again was using his brain and had a rather clear idea of what was coming.

Sultan Murad was not happy. Not only did he feel that Vlad Senior was slipping away from his influence and had started to lean back towards support of the Hungarians, but an annual tribute, paid since Vlad Senior's father Mircea, had not been paid lately.

The price for peace, and the survival of Vlad Senior's rule, was a renewal of the annual tribute, a contingent of Wallachian boys for Devsirme (a system by which the Ottomans took boys from conquered or subservient populations to be brought up as future Janissaries, the Sultan's Household Troops) and, to keep Vlad Senior honest, his sons Vlad and Radu were to remain with the Ottomans as hostages.

Young Vlad Dracula's fate here takes its first major turn. Though life as a hostage did not mean imprisonment, but rather that the boy would be further educated under the responsibility of the Ottoman court, it was not a mere formality either.

Only the year before two other brothers, sons of the Serbian despot George Brankovic, had been placed as hostages with the Ottoman court, and when the sultan suspected that their father was conspiring against him, the two brothers were blinded with hot irons.

We shall shortly come back to Vlad Dracula's years as a hostage, but let us stay with the story of Vlad Senior for now.

In the succeeding years, Vlad Senior played a dangerous, but reasonably successful double game. He apparently did not partake in aggressions against the Ottomans, while at the same time he made Wallachian troops available to the various Christian campaigns under the command of his son Mircea, but not officially under the Wallachian banner.

And the five years following Vlad Senior's peace agreement with Sultan Murad were not quiet. Already late the year after did a combined Christian army (including Wallachians under Mircea) defeat the Ottomans at Nis and recapture large parts of Bulgaria, before winter forced them back the way they had come.

The year following saw a new campaign, lead by King Ladislav III of Poland, but very much the brainchild of Janos Hunyadi. This campaign did not meet the approval of Vlad Senior; indeed he was arguing strongly that it was ill planned and undermanned. Nevertheless he once again sent Mircea with a contingent of Wallachian Cavalry. The Christian army met a crushing defeat at Varna, and King Ladislav was killed in the battle.

On his way back to Transylvania, Janos Hunyadi was intercepted by Vlad Senior to face accusations and arguments relating to the ill fated campaign, and the story goes that Vlad Senior had the tip of his sword on Hunyadi's throat during the argument. He eventually released Hunyadi, but only after having taken a ransom as a token of his displeasure. This very tense relationship with Hunyadi should eventually turn out to be fatal.

Vlad Senior did partly participate in a small expedition the following year, in which an attempt was made to find the body of King Ladislav, lost during the preceding year's battle, but again it was mainly Mircea who led the small Wallachian contingent.

In 1447 Vlad Senior and Sultan Murad renewed their peace agreement, and Hunyadi, now back on his feet, had had enough of Vlad Senior playing both sides. In November he launched an attack on Wallachia, an attack that also included buying the local Boyars to raise an internal revolt. Mircea Dracula was caught by the Boyars in Targoviste, tortured, blinded and buried alive. Vlad Senior fled, probably trying to get to the Ottomans, but he was caught close to Bucharest (at that time an insignificant village) and beheaded. Janos Hunyadi made himself regent before installing one of the many potential princes (Vladislav) on the throne.

Thus ended the life of Vlad Dracul, diplomat, warrior and one of the smarter rulers of fifteenth century Wallachia.

Hostage

As we have seen in the story of Vlad Senior, his young son Vlad Dracula became involved in politics, albeit by implication, round and about the age of ten. In effect from that point, young Vlad had little if any choice in the route his life would follow; he was a player.

At the time Vlad was handed over to the care of the Ottoman court, he would have already started his training as a knight, and it was in the nature of inter-court hostage taking that such education be continued.

Vlad would already have been a capable horseman, and he would have trained with a sword (and possibly other weapons) for a few years already, even if such weapons were smaller and lighter than the real thing. It was not uncommon that young princes of the blood had full suits of armour made to measure, so that from their early days they could adjust to the special conditions that apply to fighting in such, even though these were expensive and may have been outside the reach of the Wallachian court.

Firearms were gradually being introduced into contemporary warfare, and it is likely that Vlad would have been trained with a musket (recently adapted by the Ottoman Janissaries) as a modern supplement to more traditional arms such as the short bow, fired from horseback, that was the traditional weapon of the Ottoman light cavalry.

Where Vlad's traditional literary education would normally have included the Bible and a selection of Greek philosophy, under Ottoman supervision the Koran was the literary centrepiece and it was quietly hoped, but never officially enforced, that the pupils would decide to convert to Islam and thus form a religious bond with the Ottomans that could be exploited in the years to come.

If Vlad was aware of how dangerous it really could be to be a hostage is unknown, but he will surely have been aware of what happened to the Brankovic sons and as he grew older he would have developed a more acute awareness of his situation and its inherent dangers. He will have probably felt responsible for the safety of his younger brother, Radu, though such loyalty should show not to be reciprocal over time.

It can be assumed that Vlad would have been kept in some kind of know regarding recent events in the region, though probably in a strongly censored form.

As he grew into a teenager, he would have been given a rank, probably one of junior officer in respect of his pedigree, in the Ottoman army and he is likely to have seen combat in one of the many skirmishes that constantly developed on the borders of the Ottoman Empire.

But really, all of this is speculation and assumptions made on the basis of the stories of others in similar circumstances.

One further assumption we can make is that Vlad would have met the young Ottoman crown prince Mehmed.

Mehmed was of similar age to Vlad (born in 1432) and it is fully possible that they at times would have shared education at the palace in Edirne.

In 1444 Sultan Murad decided to abdicate and leave the throne for his then twelve year old son, though in practical terms the empire would have been run by a council lead by the Grand Vizier Halil Pasha. Exactly why he did that is still puzzling historians, but no matter his reasons, he retired to Manisa and left Mehmed and his advisers in charge. Though this would probably not have affected Vlad directly, he would have had the opportunity to see civil and military revolt at first hand as Mehmed's rule was not popular and widespread revolt took place, not least in the capital city of Edirne. The situation didn't last long, as Murad was soon forced out of retirement to meet the Christian army heading for the battle of Varna.

Ignoring the ever present and underlying element of danger, Vlad and Radu would have lived a rather privileged and protected life, similar to that of many other royal or noble youth throughout Europe, but murder, mayhem and politics was about to send Vlad off on a new journey when news came of his father's and brother's overthrow and murder. In principle the death of his father set him free, but in reality he was always a prisoner of his blood.

Sir Jens

CHAPTER 3
RULER AND REFUGEE

Sir Jens

Proposition

Who proposed to Vlad Dracula that, following his father's death, he, at the tender age of seventeen, should take the throne of Wallachia is unknown.

He could of course have come up with the idea himself, but it is unlikely that he would have made the jump from his protected life with the Ottomans to see himself as an active player in Balkan politics.

Initially, after having gotten news of his father's and brother's deaths, Vlad stayed with the Ottomans. He was free, his time as a hostage lapsed with the death of his father, but really he had nowhere to go.

The Hungarians, represented by Janos Hunyadi, would probably have had him killed like his father and elder brother and as he had only ever lived at the Wallachian or Ottoman courts, staying put was the obvious option.

The world, however, was turning and only the year after having secured Wallachia for a pliant ruler, Janos Hunyadi waged war on the Ottomans again. This time he led a large Christian army through Serbia to battle in Kosovo, in an attempt to face off and defeat the main Ottoman army once and for all. The ensuing battle took place at the same place as a similar battle fought in 1389, and thus became known as the second Battle of Kosovo.

It is known that the Ottoman crown prince Mehmed saw battle for the first time here, and it is very likely that Vlad Dracula would also have fought in this battle under the Ottoman banner as he was by now a fully trained officer and no friend of Janos Hunyadi who had recently orchestrated the murder of his father and elder brother.

The Christian army was destroyed in an (atypical) two-day battle and Janos Hunyadi narrowly escaped, only to be taken prisoner by George Brankovic, the despot of Serbia, who wanted to show the sultan who's side he was on and who anyhow didn't like Janos at all (or indeed the fact that his troops had looted all the way through Serbia on their way to Kosovo). With Janos Hunyadi was Vladislav, the Voivode of Wallachia, and while being held prisoners in the Serbian capital of Smederevo their fate was unknown and they were feared dead.

Power vacuums like that were rarely left for long in the fifteenth century, and this one was no exception. With a Hungarian supported Voivode in Wallachia, and the possible death of both him and his powerful protector, I believe that the opportunity was just too good for the Ottoman court not to react. But they needed a suitable candidate for the presumed empty throne, and they didn't have to search far before someone came up with a suitable name; Vlad Dracula!

So rather than what has been suggested by some historians, namely that a power-hungry and vengeful Vlad Dracula convinced the sultan to give him troops so he could go to Wallachia and avenge his father and brother, I think that it was the Sultan whom proposed to Vlad Dracula that perhaps now was the time, and promised him the necessary support.

First Rule

In the summer of 1448 Vlad Dracula led a small Ottoman force into Wallachia and marched unopposed on Targoviste. Those Boyars that had not been killed at Kosovo were not in a position to put up any kind of fight, so in October, Vlad Dracula became Vlad III of Wallachia, he was seventeen years old and already at the top, but it would soon enough all come tumbling down.

Though elected by the Boyars as the ruler, it was of course mainly due to the presence of his Ottoman troops and really only on the assumption that Voivode Vladislav had died at Kosovo, and others too would remind him of that.

The Hungarian vice-governor of Transylvania wrote to him and suggested that he should come and stay with him in Brasov until the fate of Janos Hunyadi, and implicit Voivode Vladislav, was determined, but Vlad refused (leaving us the first letter signed by him), arguing that if he left Wallachia now, the (victorious) Ottomans would put someone else on the throne, and that if Hunyadi should turn out to be alive then `we will meet him and we will make peace with him`.

Over and above this, there are no records of any real activity during this first reign of Vlad Dracula. With winter setting in, a less than friendly environment in which he is mainly seen as an opportunistic usurper and with only a small contingent of Ottoman troops (probably eager to go home) to protect him, I envisage him holed up in the palace in Targoviste, waiting for final word on the fate of Janos Hunyadi and Vladislav.

What he probably did was take the opportunity to gather the best possible intelligence on what really happened when his father and brother were killed, and to the extent he did not already know the details, it would not have left him with any warm feelings toward Janos Hunyadi or the ever shifty Boyars of Wallachia.

He didn't have to wait long though, because already in December, after Vlad had been Voivode of Wallachia for only two months or so, Janos Hunyadi and Vladislav returned from their captivity. Petru II of Moldavia declared himself in support of them and Vlad had not only lost the moral high ground, now that it was clear that Vladislav was alive, but he was utterly outgunned and politically outmanoeuvred.

With his now more exact knowledge of Janos Hunyadi's role in his father's and brother's murder, he decided not to 'meet him and make peace with him' after all, but rather do the only smart thing; run!

Refugee

Vlad, with his Ottoman troops, went back to Edirne and the Ottoman court. He needed to make sure he was on good terms with the sultan, so at least he had one less potential enemy to worry about. It is not known how the sultan reacted to the news that once again Wallachia was, effectively, under Hungarian control, but there is no record of any blame being put onto Vlad.

He didn't, however, stay, but left the relative safety of the Ottoman court to take his chances and live as a refugee and Vlad's whereabouts for the seven years between early 1449 and 1456 are only very sketchily known.

To get an idea of where he was we need to look at the person he had turned into when he once again returns into mainstream history and the contemporary events that could have formed him so.

By the time Vlad begins his second, and most famous, rule in 1456, he is a sly politician and warlord, though not necessarily the best of diplomats. Somewhere along the way, in the intervening seven years he must had gained the experience, confidence and savvy that he was without at the time of his first, short, rule.

Though the details are weak (women playing little part in official chronicles of the time), it is known that Vlad Senior (Dracul) had married a daughter of the Moldavian Voivode Alexandru Cel Bun (The Good). That didn't mean that she was necessarily Vlad Dracula's mother, but the family connection was close enough for Vlad to be considered family by her brother Bogdan (II), the new ruler of Moldavia, making the Moldavian court in Suceava one of the few places Vlad could safely go, so that is where he went after leaving the Ottoman court (presumably on good terms) sometime in 1449.

In Suceava he met and befriended his cousin, the later ruler of Moldavia, Stefan (to become known as Cel Mare, or The Great) who was of similar age. This friendship would form a bond between the two that was to be thoroughly tested over the years to come.

Now having tasted politics, Vlad would have taken the opportunity to follow the intrigues of the Moldavian court at close hand, and it only lasted till late 1451 until he learned yet another lesson in contemporary statecraft, a lesson that nearly cost him his life.

Voivode Bogdan's brother, Petru Aron, had his eyes on the Moldavian throne, and in October 1451 he conspired with the local Boyars. One of the Moldavian Boyar's was getting married and Voivode Bogdan, accompanied by his son Stefan and (it can be assumed) Vlad, was the guest of honour. The Boyar who was getting married was however part of Petru Aron's conspiracy and they took the opportunity to attack and behead Bogdan, sending Stefan and Vlad fleeing for their lives. This time, out of options, they headed for neighbouring Transylvania.

The new Voivode of Moldavia was leaning towards support for Poland, rather than Hungary, so Stefan had little to fear from the Hungarians and Janos Hunyadi. Vlad, however, was still not popular, following his coup a couple of years earlier. Nevertheless he and Stefan ended up in the Saxon city of Brasov in Southern Transylvania.

Janos Hunyadi had lost some of his former power following his defeat at Kosovo. He was no longer Governor of Transylvania, but he still held the castle of Hunedoara and had sufficient power remaining to stay involved in local politics. His former protégé, Voivode Vladislav of Wallachia, had reacted to Janos' fall from grace by breaking out of their alliance and start leaning towards the Ottomans. Janos in turn reacted by occupying the duchies of Fagaras and Amlas (physically located in Transylvania but part of Wallachia), making the break between them complete.

When news of Vlad Dracula's appearance in Brasov got to Janos, he demanded that the city hand him over, and Vlad had to flee again, this time to the neighbouring town of Sibiu. While he was there, and not unlikely brokered by Stefan, a truce was found between Vlad Dracula and Janos Hunyadi.

Vlad was received by Janos at his castle in Hunedoara and later at the Hungarian court in Buda, where he was accompanying Janos at the official crowning of King Vladislav in 1452.

Through the influence of Janos, Vlad received a title as "Defender of Transylvania", effectively a waiting position as a glorified march-warden, and was given quarters in Sibiu. Though still not welcome in his native country of Wallachia, he now had his back pretty well free, and could focus on improving his skills before he once again could make a bid for Wallachia.

The events in Moldavia and Wallachia, as important to Vlad as they were, were however just sideshows to the bigger events of the time, and Vlad's contemporary opportunities to further learn statecraft and warfare were galore.

Skanderbeg

George Kastrioti was born to a noble family in Albania (then under Ottoman rule) in 1405. At a young age he was handed over to the Ottomans as a hostage, in circumstances not dissimilar to those of Vlad Dracula four decades later.

George was trained as an army officer, and became a very successful commander in the Ottoman army. He was given the name Iskender Bey (Lord Alexander), which in its Latin version became Skanderbeg.

For reasons outside the scope of this story, Skanderbeg turned sides in 1443. He went back to his native Albania where he united the local fractions under a single anti-Ottoman banner.

For the decades to follow, he fought the Ottomans in Albania, at various times being more successful than at others, but consistently being a thorn in the side of the Ottomans and preventing them from taking control of the Adriatic coast, a prerequisite for their desire for a move on Italy.

In a scenario similar to Von Blücher's reinforcement of Wellington's army at the Battle of Waterloo nearly 400 years later, Skanderbeg was on his way with reinforcements to the second Battle of Kosovo in 1448. In his rather brash manner, Janos Hunyadi however decided to open the battle without him and even though the battle proper lasted two days, Skanderbeg's reinforcements only arrived after the battle had been lost, and all they could do was cover the back of the fleeing Christian army. As the battle was a very close affair, mainly decided by sheer numbers, it is very likely that if Skanderbeg had reached the battle in time (or Hunyadi had postponed hostilities accordingly), then the Christian army would have won the battle, the same way

Wellington's army finally defeated Napoleon only due to the last-moment arrival of Von Blücher's Prussian reinforcements.

A Christian victory at Kosovo would have opened up the Balkans to a Christian re-conquest. But as it was, Skanderbeg returned to Albania to fight the Ottomans on his own.

Being consistently out-numbered by the vast resources at the disposal of the Ottomans, Skanderbeg developed and deployed a highly efficient guerrilla warfare model, avoiding open battle and using his troops' intimate knowledge of the local terrain to their best advantage. Despite the overwhelming odds, he kept the Ottomans at bay until his death in 1468. A decade later, Albania was once again under Ottoman control.

If the Christian army had won the second Battle of Kosovo, then the Ottomans would not have sent Vlad Dracula off to take the Wallachian throne in 1448 and his journey would have been dramatically different, but as it was, the circumstances created learning ground for Vlad Dracula.

There is no evidence that Vlad Dracula ever met Skanderbeg. By the time Vlad was a hostage at the Ottoman court, Skanderbeg was already fighting the Ottomans in Albania, but it doesn't need to end with that.

As there is little record of what Vlad Dracula did to occupy himself and improve his skills, between 1452 and 1456, it is far from impossible that he would have gone and joined Skanderbeg for a period of time to learn the art of guerrilla warfare.

His motivation to do so could well have been inspired by the actions of his grandfather, Mircea Cel Batran, who was famous for his defence of Wallachia in 1394, where Sultan Bayazid I invaded with an army that outnumbered

Mircea's forced four to one. Mircea deployed guerrilla warfare, starved the enemy and only engaged them in raids until a final battle took place in a swampy area (of Mircea's choosing) where the Ottomans could not spread their army wide and thus could not utilise their numeric superiority. For military-history buffs; this is similar to the way Alexander the Great chose the ground for the Battle of Issus in 332 BC.

Vlad would have known by now that should he regain the throne of Wallachia, then he would in all likelihood have to fight the Ottomans at some time or other, so even if he didn't actively join Skanderbeg in Albania, then there is no doubt that Skanderbeg would have set an example to Vlad by providing a model for fighting the Ottomans without open battle, an approach Vlad most definitely mastered ten years later when it did become his turn to fight a numerically superior Ottoman army on his home soil. He picked this skill up somewhere, and I believe it was from Skanderbeg (though the romantic in me would like to think it was from Alexander the Great).

Mehmed II

In 1451, about the time Vlad and Stefan were refugees in Transylvania, Sultan Murad II died, and his son Mehmed became Sultan Mehmed II.

In the process he had his (only surviving) younger brother killed, and he would later make fratricide a matter of law with the words 'Whichever of my sons inherits the sultan's throne, it behoves him to kill his brothers in the interest of world order'.

At nineteen years of age and having behind him already a rather unsuccessful, albeit short, reign during his father's abdication in 1444, the Christian World took a deep breath of relief. The general belief was that this new boy-sultan was inexperienced, unpopular and incompetent, a belief soon reinforced by Mehmed's instant eagerness to sign peace agreements with all and sundry.

However, despite the opinion of his adversaries, Mehmed is far from incompetent, rather he is capable and ready and he has a plan. He is going to do what many have attempted before and failed to do. He is going to kill off the Byzantine Empire once and for all; he is going to conquer Constantinople.

Having secured peace agreements with his more dangerous neighbours, who were so convinced of his incompetence that they happily took their eyes off him, Mehmed starts moving, and moving fast.

First he builds a new fortress on the European side of the Bosporus Strait, opposite an older fortress on the Anatolian side built by his great grandfather Bayezid I. With the technology of cannons now advanced to a stage where it was becoming controllable and predictable, he installs cannons on either side of the narrow strait and effectively seals off access to Constantinople from the Black Sea. The new fortress is called the Throat Cutter (Boğazkesen), playing on the local name for the Bosporus Strait as "The Throat" and the strangling effect it's closure had on Constantinople. The new castle was built in only four months and sixteen days, to Mehmed's own design, and it still stands today.

Having now prevented reinforcements from reaching Constantinople from the Black Sea, Mehmed sent an expedition force into Peloponnese (Southern Greece) to keep the only Byzantine fighting force outside of Constantinople itself occupied.

In the spring of 1453, with the Christian states in the West ignoring the Byzantine emperor's desperate appeals for help, Mehmed moved his fleet into position around Constantinople and his land army from Edirne to the land walls of Constantinople. These walls, consistently maintained, improved and expanded had protected Constantinople successfully from conquest by land for a thousand years. Many, including the Ottomans, had tried, all had failed, but Mehmed wasn't deterred and he embraced the latest in military technology; siege cannons with which to break down the walls.

Inside the city of Constantinople a desperately small force was trying to defend an impossibly long wall, with the Throat Cutter and the sizeable Ottoman fleet keeping further reinforcements by sea at bay.

Adding further complication was the Emperor's last ditch attempt to get support from the Pope by accepting a unification of the Eastern (Orthodox) and Western (Catholic) churches, a move that was enormously unpopular with the local population and dealt a serious blow to the morale of the city's defenders.

The fall of Constantinople

I am not going to retell the story of the siege, and conquest, of Constantinople. Others have done it in detail I could only dream of mastering, and I in particular recommend Roger Crowley's "1453".

I shall instead stay with the effects on history in general and the life of Vlad Dracula in particular.

When Mehmed's army conquered Constantinople on 29 May 1453, it was the effective end of the Byzantine Empire, though disparate enclaves still remained to be mopped up in the years following.

Up to this point most Western military commanders, including Janos Hunyadi, had believed that a single big battle won could force the Ottomans back across the narrow straits to Anatolia, but with the symbol of Christian civilisation and heritage overnight becoming the showpiece of Ottoman supremacy, the last remnants of that dream disappeared.

Constantinople became Istanbul and acted as capital of the Ottoman Empire for nearly 500 years, until the modern day Turkish Republic took Ankara as its capital in 1923.

The Christian world was thrown into a frenzy of panic and predictions of doom and gloom. Though most Christian rulers had for centuries ignored the more and more desperate cries for help from various emperors in Constantinople, and placidly, if not even with some ill hidden schadenfreude, watched the formed empire shrink into a shadow of its former glory, its demise suddenly made the Christian World realise that the Ottoman threat was there to stay, and that it wouldn't take that much for the Ottomans to push through to Western Europe itself.

Many conferences were had. Some rulers agreed on active warfare (the Pope himself trying to revitalise the former Crusader spirit), some didn't. Those that did agree made promises of troops, few delivered. Lots of talking along the lines of `someone should do something` was had, but nothing much materialised. For the more cynical observer it is not that different from watching the UN trying to agree on anything in the twenty-first Century.

Where was Vlad when Constantinople fell? Well this is probably one of the battles he missed. He is unlikely to have fought on the Ottoman side (though a good part of the Ottoman army was made up of non indigenous troops and the master behind the siege cannons was Saxon-Hungarian), as that would have put him on a very bad footing with the Hungarians. He is equally unlikely to have fought on the Christian side, as few reinforcements made it through the Ottoman blockade and those that did were mainly annihilated in, or after, the battle itself.

The follow up to the fall of Constantinople, and Mehmed II's emergence as Fatih (The Conqueror), would however soon set of the next part of Vlad Dracula's story.

The Siege of Belgrade

It did not take long for the Hungarians to realise that despite all the talking, they were effectively alone in defending the Christian World against the Ottoman expansion.

Though Mehmed immediately following the conquest of Constantinople focused on mopping up the last Byzantine remains in Greece and the Mediterranean, including an unsuccessful attempt at throwing the Knights of Rhodes out of Rhodes, his ambition was clear; he wanted to once and for all break Hungarian resistance and break through to Western Europe. The place to do just that was Belgrade.

Belgrade, at that time, was Hungarian (the contemporary capital of Serbia being Smederevo). If the Ottomans could break through at Belgrade, then the door was wide open for them to not only swarm all over Hungary, but effectively continue straight into the heartland of Christianity.

Situated at the confluence of two rivers (the Danube and the Sava), Belgrade was protected by extensive walls and a massive castle, a setup not that different from Constantinople, so Mehmed thought he had the formula at hand for a successful siege and conquest.

The Hungarians were well aware of where an attack was likely to take place, but they had little in terms of troops to muster against the massive and high spirited Ottoman army. They took new measures in use and recruited peasant soldiers in their thousands, as well as they invited volunteers from all over Europe to come as reinforcements. Adding to these they sent an army of app. 10,000 professional soldiers, bringing the total number of defenders to more than 50,000, substantially more than had defended Constantinople and under the command of the veteran Janos Hunyadi.

With a besieging army surrounding the walls, the defenders were dependent on being able to reinforce and resupply Belgrade across the Danube River, so Mehmed repeated the strategy he had previously deployed at Constantinople; he started hostilities in the spring of 1456 with a naval blockade. The Turkish fleet, numbering 200 ships, sailed up the Danube and were chained together to form a barrier across the rivers, preventing the Hungarians from ferrying troops and supplies into the besieged city.

That done, his main army arrived in front of the walls of Belgrade, numbering more than 100,000 troops, potentially as many as 300,000, though contemporary sources are utterly unreliable in that regard. With him he also brought siege cannons, so successfully deployed before the walls of Constantinople, or rather the even newer advance in military technology; the capability to cast cannons locally from raw materials - much easier transported than the finished cannons themselves.

Like at Constantinople, Mehmed's strategy was to use the cannons to make breaches in the walls and then send mass infantry attacks into the breaches and overwhelm the defenders with sheer firepower and numbers.

But Janos Hunyadi had learned from Constantinople as well, and had as his priority number one to break the Turkish naval blockade. He successfully deployed a Hungarian navy in battle with the, immobile, Ottoman navy and managed to break the blockade and keep the critical supply-route across the Danube open.

That didn't prevent the Ottomans from continuing their assault on the walls, and soon big breaches started to appear. Mehmed's strategy seemed to be working again, and the defenders became more and more desperate, trying to repair and defend multiple breaches in the walls.

On 21 July, Mehmed ordered an all-out assault on the walls and even though it was ultimately repelled (amongst other means by pouring flammable materials into the moat and setting it on fire), it was clear that the situation was becoming critical and the attackers could only be repelled so many times before they broke through. Once again, this was a direct copy of the situation at Constantinople, where the Ottomans launched several all-out attacks before the final breakthrough was achieved.

After a quiet day on the 22 July, where the Ottomans were busy recovering their (many) dead from the preceding day's battle and the Hungarians were busy ferrying supplies across the river, something strange happened on 23 July that would change the history of the world, more by chance than by design.

Appreciating the need for every single available hand in the consistent defence and repair of the walls, Janos Hunyadi had issued strict orders that the defenders were not to venture outside the walls and engage the Ottomans. Despite this, a small contingent of the rather undisciplined defenders decided to ignore this order and go outside to harass the Ottomans, now occupied by burying their dead and reorganising.

The small contingent of defenders started shouting insults at the Ottomans, and some starting shooting arrows at them. When the Ottomans did not respond, more joined, more insults were shouted and more arrows were fired. Once again the Ottomans did not respond, so more joined in, and the small contingent became a crowd. Spurred on by the passiveness of the Ottomans, the crowd became more aggressive and started to advance on the Ottomans, leading to even more joining in, and ultimately what had started as a bit of a brawl became a full scale attack, finally joined by Janos Hunyadi and the army proper.

The Ottomans never saw it coming, and by the time they did they were being overwhelmed. The Christian troops, now in frenzy, went straight through the, thin, Ottoman defences and the Ottoman army did something untypical; they ran.

Mehmed himself was wounded and rendered unconscious, and was hastily brought away from harm's way, and the Ottoman army went into full flight, harassed by the attacking Christian forces who hacked them down in the thousands.

The Christian did not press their advantage, but returned to behind the walls, not realising that they had won the battle, but rather thinking that they had at best bought themselves some time. An Ottoman comeback, however, never materialised, the Ottoman fleet sailed off, and the remnants of the Army sneaked off in the night and returned to Edirne, harassed all the way by Serbian troops that took the opportunity to further decimate their numbers.

The Ottomans lost an estimated 75,000 men in the battle and the following flight, an enormous number that put a serious dent in Mehmed's ambitions for a while. Mehmed himself was devastated and popular history has it that he had to be forcefully prevented from taking poison in his despair. He would however bounce back later.

Vlad Dracula did not take part in the defence of Belgrade. He had been ordered to stay in Transylvania and protect the border from raids by Ottoman or Wallachian raiding-parties, as the Wallachian Voivode, Vladislav, by now had turned fully pro-Ottoman and Vlad, after all, held the title of Protector of Transylvania.

The Ottoman defeat at Belgrade however set the stage for Vlad's next move; once again he was going for the throne of Wallachia.

CHAPTER 4
SURVIVOR

Sir Jens

Opportunity

When Sultan Mehmed's Ottoman army is defeated before Belgrade in July 1456, it represents a new opportunity for Vlad Dracula. This time he doesn't need anyone to put the idea to him. He is ready; indeed he has probably been so for a good while.

The Voivode of Wallachia, Vladislav, has over the years strayed from his former alliance with Hungary and, the victor of Belgrade, Janos Hunyadi. He is by 1456 for all intents and purposes a full Ottoman vassal, and with the serious setback suffered by the Ottomans at Belgrade, he is vulnerable and without support.

For four years, since 1452, Vlad has held the title of Protector of Transylvania, with quarters in Sibiu provided by the Hungarian King. In this capacity Vlad would have the command of a small military force; big enough to stop raids across the border, but not big enough for a full scale campaign.

It is likely that he over the years started to build up a group of loyal (to him) Wallachians whom for one reason of the other found themselves exiled, and whom would have seen Vlad Dracula as a rallying point. They would have made up his household troops, and may well have included some who were more political than warlike and who could advise Vlad on matters political and diplomatic.

Stefan of Moldavia was still with him, and it is equally likely that, like Vlad, he would have built up his own household troops from exiled Moldavians.

After the Siege of Belgrade, Vlad got the word 'go' from the victorious Janos Hunyadi, who had no warm feelings left for Voivode Vladislav, and Vlad gathered what troops he could get his hands on and was off to Wallachia.

This time, however, there was some resistance. Vladislav mustered his own troops and the two opposing forces fought it out near the Wallachian capital of Targoviste. The details are sparse, but Vlad must have won the day because at the end of August Vladislav was killed.

And here the tales and legends start! By which I mean that up to this point, the story of Vlad Dracula has been either reasonably factual or purely speculative. Once popular tales and legends begin to emerge, then it becomes very difficult to determine what is fact, what is speculation, what is wishful thinking and what is just outright made up.

The legend goes that Vladislav was killed in hand to hand battle with Vlad and whereas I am not saying that didn't happen, I am saying that as is the case with practically all the legends, the event is historical (i.e. Vladislav is killed) but the details are unsubstantiated (i.e. he was killed in hand-to-hand combat with Vlad). As we move on I will specifically note when we are talking about legend and when we are not. Over and above the legend there is also a range of written stories, which I shall ignore for now and deal with separately in chapter seven.

Whether by Vlad's hand or otherwise, Vladislav was killed in the fight for Wallachia and Vlad once again ruled in Targoviste. With no resistance left, he was once again elected Voivode of Wallachia. Contrary to when that same thing happened eight years earlier, this time he had a plan.

Friend and Foe

Vlad's first priority would have been simple; survival! He had by now been involved in, or witnessed, enough coups to understand that life at the top can be very short. To survive you have to first and foremost understand whom are your friends and whom are your enemies, so let's have a look at how that would have looked for Vlad Dracula when he re-emerged at the throne of Wallachia in September 1456.

His friends were easily counted. His cousin Stefan of Moldavia was with him, and had been since they fled Moldavia together five years prior. Stefan was a good friend and ally, but had nothing much to add in terms of actual power. Furthermore, Stefan didn't stay for long. Already in 1457 did Vlad help him with a contingent of 6,000 Wallachian cavalry-men, and Stefan went back to Moldavia to successfully overthrow his uncle Petru Aron and become Stefan III of Moldavia. He should later be given the moniker "Cel Mare" (The Great).

The powerful Hungarian baron Janos Hunyadi, though responsible for the murder of Vlad's father's and brother's deaths had, in a paradoxical turn of events, turned into the real power behind Vlad. It was on Hunyadi's (rather than the Hungarian King's) orders that Vlad had marched on Targoviste and taken the throne.

The most powerful potential enemies would be the two mighty neighbouring empires.

Even though Vlad had re-taken the throne by killing the Ottoman vassal-Voivode, the Ottomans were not in good shape after their recent defeat, and had other more pressing matters at hand that getting involved in Wallachia - Unless he directly provoked them, Vlad could, for the time being, feel reasonably safe in terms of the Ottomans, not least so if he kept up payment of the annual tribute already agreed during his father's rule.

The Hungarians were a mixed bag. By the time Vlad had secured his throne, Janos Hunyadi had died at Belgrade, taken by plague. Janos's death had thrown Hungary into a de-facto civil war, and there was a chance that King Ladislav of Hungary would see Vlad as "Hunyadi's man". The threat was not imminent, but it had to be dealt with sooner rather than later.

Next on the list were the Wallachian Boyars. Now they were a different story altogether. Vlad knew the role they had played in the overthrow and murder of his father and elder brother (and numerous other former rulers). He had also seen the Boyars of Moldavia murder his uncle, Bogdan, and he had himself witnessed how the Boyars would readily change allegiance depending on the most likely winner, or the deepest pockets. Though currently he, seemingly, had the support of the Boyars, he could have had no confidence in their lasting loyalty and if anyone was an immediate, and for that matter long-term, threat to him it was most probably his own Boyars. We shall see how he dealt with that shortly.

Third on the list would be the Saxon merchant-cities of Transylvania. As previously discussed they were sensitive to who ruled Wallachia in order that they were given trade rights and tax concessions, and they had no qualms in getting involved in coups. Indeed they would often nurture yet another royal potential just in case they needed a friendly Voivode. In addition their pockets were deep, so they were fully capable of buying the Boyars as and when required. The Saxon cities were a definite threat, though not necessarily immediately, so they had to be dealt with too and as we shall see in following; dealt with they were.

But like Vlad himself, let us deal with the enemies in turn!

The Boyars

The most immediate threat to Vlad Dracula came from his own Boyars, and in dealing with that threat, Vlad for the first time shows what kind of man he has become.

Vlad could have waited, perhaps tried to make an assessment of who was friend and who was foe, perhaps tried to build up some kind of real loyalty from the Boyars, but that was not his style. The Vlad Dracula that now emerged after eight years of studying the events around him had a very clear idea of how to deal with potential enemies. You strike first, you strike fast and you strike hard.

So according to legend, Vlad got the Boyars together for Easter 1457, at the palace in Targoviste. At the ensuing feast he casually asked if any of the Boyars knew how many rulers Wallachia had during their lifetime. Those who didn't know, and that was the vast majority, were impaled in the courtyard of the palace, with their families. And those that weren't impaled were put in irons, again with their families, and marched to Poienari to work as slave-workers on the renovation of the hilltop castle 'until their clothes fell off their backs'.

Right! Or then again; perhaps not.

That Vlad confronted the Boyars is without question. That he had some of them killed is unquestionable. That some were put in irons and marched off to Poienari is definitely possible. That some families were completely eradicated is equally probable. What is not so very probable is that he in effect eradicated the complete boyar class in one swift move. Indeed we shall later see that some of the Boyars managed to flee Transylvania and gather in Brasov, remerging as supporters of Vlad's rival Dan.

Even though Vlad is known for having put "his own men", presumably from his group of exile followers, in place of the missing Boyars, eradicating the complete boyar class would have thrown the country into a level of turmoil that would have been catastrophic and potentially have set him on a direct collision course with the Hungarians, as there were many family and dynastic connections across the border of Wallachia and Transylvania.

Instead, in my opinion, Vlad here shows what would become his trademark; the brutal sacrifice of the few as an example to the many.

If you want to kill someone, then impalement is not the fastest, less resource demanding or indeed the most efficient method. Impalement, like crucifixion, only serves one single purpose; to strike terror into the spectators. It is a means to discourage others from doing whatever the poor recipient of this most barbaric treatment has done.

Vlad could have just, say, beheaded them, but that would not have had the psychological shock-effect that impalement has. He knew this, he had seen it work, because despite the fact that it is Vlad Dracula that has over time become the symbol of impalement, and indeed was given the moniker "Tepes" (The Impaler), he didn't invent impalement, it was something he had learned while in the care of the Ottomans.

The Ottomans used impalement as the showcase choice of execution the same way the Romans used crucifixion. One example that fits in the timeframe is related to the Throat Cutter castle that was mentioned earlier. In November of 1452, when the castle was still new, a Venetian captain, Antonio Rizzo, decided to try to run his ship through the Ottoman blockade and land his shipment of food in Constantinople. His ship was hit by a cannonball and sunk. He and his surviving crew were arrested when they reached the shore and brought in front of the sultan in Edirne. Despite pleas from the Venetian ambassador, Sultan Mehmed wanted to make certain that it was understood what would happen to anyone that dared try to break his blockade. The surviving sailors were beheaded but captain Rizzo was impaled 'by a stake though his anus'. A couple of sailors were, however, saved and sent to Constantinople to tell the story!

Back to the Boyars. Like Mehmed in the story above, Vlad would have probably selected a few Boyars, and perhaps some of their family members, for impalement as an example to the rest. It is not unreasonable to assume that those singled out for this special treatment were those Boyars directly involved in the murder of Vlad's father and elder brother.

Equally, he could well have selected some, and their families, for slave labour, both as a punishment in itself, but also to demonstrate to all and sundry that a new sheriff had come to town, and his law would be applied equally to high and low. And in this he starts his journey towards popular hero of the people.

His behaviour is far from unique. To eradicate the leading elements of the old regime (and their families) is a repetitive theme throughout history. Only sixty odd years later, in 1540, the same scenario was enacted by the Danish King Christian II. Having successfully conquered Sweden, he invited the Swedish nobility, church leaders and other dignitaries to a peace and reconciliation feast at the castle in Stockholm. Once they were all inside he had the doors barred and trumped up accusations read out. With a few exceptions they were found guilty (of heresy as it was, by questioning his divine right to the throne) and they were led off and beheaded. A recorded total of eighty-two people were executed, and this is probably the kind of numbers we should also be looking at in the case of Vlad's decimation, rather than eradication, of the Wallachian Boyars.

As far as anyone knows, Vlad had no more trouble with the Wallachian Boyars, and he could now concentrate on the next threat, the Saxon cities of Transylvania.

Hungarian Intrigue

Shortly following his successful defence of Belgrade, Janos Hunyadi died from plague. It is said that his dying words were:

> *'Defend, my friends, Christendom and Hungary from all enemies... Do not quarrel among yourselves. If you should waste your energies in altercations, you will seal your own fate as well as dig the grave of our country.'*

Whether he really said that, or others have later put the words in his mouth with 20/20 hindsight; this was good advice, and it was duly ignored.

King Ladislav Posthumous of Hungary was not a popular king. He was considered a foreigner, being a Habsburg and related the Holy Roman Emperor Frederich III, as well as weak and mainly ignorant to the Ottoman threat. An example of this is the fact that he, convinced of an impending defeat at Belgrade, fled to Vienna and left the defence to Janos Hunyadi and whatever troops he could muster.

Opposing King Ladislav was a group of Hungarian nobles, spearheaded by Janos Hunyadi, but with clear and present danger from the Ottomans, the internal struggle was contained to bickering and positioning.

Once the Ottomans had been sent packing from Belgrade and with Janos Hunyadi (and his voice of reason as above) dead, the conflict however broke into open revolt.

Janos Hunyadi's oldest son, Ladislav Hunyadi took over command of the army from his deceased father and he had the king's strong supporter Count Ulrich of Cilli murdered in Belgrade, a move designed to make himself a candidate for the Hungarian throne. Ladislav Hunyadi was, however, captured and beheaded and his younger brother, Matthias, was imprisoned.

This made the already unpopular king, now without his key supporter, so unpopular that he had to flee the country to Prague (he also held the title as King of Bohemia) where he suddenly died, probably from leukaemia, in November of 1457.

Another party supporting King Vladislav was the Saxon city-states of Transylvania, and this is where Vlad suddenly become involved in Hungary's internal affairs.

I have mentioned earlier that with the conflict in Hungary, there was a clear risk that Vlad would be seen as "Hunyadi's man", whether he really held any loyalties to Janos Hunyadi's party or not, and that King Ladislav's party might decide to replace him with a man of their own choice.

With Ladislav Hunyadi executed and his younger brother in prison, the party opposing King Ladislav was now spearheaded by Janos Hunyadi's brother in law, Mihai Szilagy. In the midst of the ensuing chaos, the Saxon town of Bistrita, a town to far north in Transylvania to normally catch the immediate interest of Vlad Dracula, rose in revolt against Mihai Szilagy in the summer of 1457. Mihai now called in his debts, which meant that he asked Vlad Dracula for help.

Vlad now had to make a decision. He could try to solve his relationship with King Vladislav by means of diplomacy, or he could declare against the King and come in support of Mihai Szilagy. Vlad chose the latter, so with the Boyars under control and his power base secured at home, off he went to Bistrita.

The combined forces of Mihai and Vlad sacked the town, killed indiscriminately and burnt the houses of the ringleaders. Having now paid his debts, Vlad went back to Wallachia.

As it happened, Vlad had chosen the winning side, as with the death of King Ladislav a couple of months later, it was the second son of Janos Hunyadi, Mathias, who was elected King of Hungary. The risk from Hungary was now eliminated, and Vlad could turn his attention to his other enemies.

Murder and Mayhem

Having removed the most immediate threats to his life and rule, it was now time to deal with the Saxon city-states across the border in Transylvania, and as we shall see later, this move would forever link the name Vlad Dracula and Transylvania in a manner that has obscured the real story over the centuries to follow.

The Saxon city-states of Transylvania, and in particular the cities of Brasov and Sibiu situated close to the border between Wallachia and Transylvania, were historically not short of getting themselves involved in coups in Transylvania and effectively nurturing their own pliant rulers as a contingency.

Vlad's participation in the sacking of Bistrita in the summer of 1457 made the Saxon cities of Transylvania aware that he was not necessarily good for business, so they started activating their own contingency plans.

The city of Sibiu started to openly nurture Vlad "Calugarul" (The Monk), a half-brother of Vlad, who would eventually get to rule Wallachia after Vlad's death.

Brasov nurtured Dan, the brother of Vlad's predecessor Vladislad and of the competing Danesti dynasty. The city-fathers in Brasov even went as far as having Dan crowned as Voivode of Wallachia and provided him with a "capital in exile" on the Timpa hill just outside the city walls.

Vlad, being aware of the potential danger from the Saxon cities, now had had enough. It was time to sort things out.

First he hit the Saxons merchants where he knew they would hurt the most, in the purse. He negated former trade agreements and forced Saxon merchants, already in Wallachia, to sell their goods at below-cost prices. He followed this up with letters, urging the Saxon cities to hand over his rivals and stop conspiring against him. As much as it hurt the Saxons, it didn't stop them, so more drastic methods were required.

In the summer of 1458, the year after his raid on Bistrita, and with Hungary (formally the overlords of the Saxon city-states) licking their wounds after their own internal strife, Vlad crossed the border to Transylvania.

First target was Sibiu. Vlad raided a number of villages around Sibiu and killed what he regarded to be supporters of his half-brother Vlad Calugarul. Exactly how he established who were, and who were not, supporters of his half-brother is unclear, and likely he just killed indiscriminately. Some of the villages were burned and completely destroyed.

In addition to this direct attack, Vlad now rounded up the remaining Saxon traders in Wallachia, accused them of not complying with his instructions of selling their goods below-cost, and had them impaled by the roadside. He furthermore rounded up a number of other Saxons in Wallachia, who he considered to be spies (even though the Saxons claimed that 'they were there to learn the language') and had them executed as well.

This was enough of a provocation for the Hungarians to intervene. The young Hungarian King Mathias sent envoys to Vlad and to Brasov, brokering a fragile peace according to which Vlad should restore the former trade agreements (and stop killing the traders), whereas Brasov should hand over Dan and those Boyars that had assembled around him (supposedly Boyars whom had managed to escape Vlad's wrath).

For all the good intentions, the peace didn't hold as Dan was still parading as Dan III on the Timpa Hill outside Brasov.

Vlad, having already tried one set of shock-tactics decided to take it a step further. If Dan wasn't coming to him, he was coming to Dan.

In the winter of 1459, Vlad quietly massed his troops near Bran on the Wallachian side of the border and within striking distance of Brasov. Riding under cover of a long and dark winter night, his forces rode on Brasov and struck in the early hours of the morning.

First target was Timpa Hill, protected by a wooden stockade which was burned down. The general assumption was made than anyone found in the Timpa Hill area were supporters of Dan, so they were rounded up and impaled at the bottom of the hill.

Next, Vlad penetrated into Brasov itself, burned the Church of St. Bartholomew, executed some of the inhabitants and looted the rest.

Dan and his loyal Boyars had however fled before Vlad got there, and had taken possession of the counties of Fagaras and Amlas, Wallachian possessions even though geographically positioned in Transylvania.

Vlad withdrew to Wallachia, and now Dan decided to settle the score. He went back to Brasov, gathered troops (supposedly with support of Brasov) and marched south-west into Wallachia. He got as far as Rucar in the Carpathian Mountains where Vlad was waiting for him.

The battle was short, Dan was probably outnumbered and ambushed and he was killed. Legend has it he was forced to dig his own grave before Vlad, personally, decapitated him. Given Vlad's aim to shock that is possibly even true.

The merchants of Brasov now got the message at last. They sent an embassy to negotiate a new peace treaty, but they were held at Targoviste as Vlad had unfinished business to close before he was ready to talk peace.

The remaining supporters of Dan, and of Vlad's half-brother Vlad Calugarul, had gathered at Amlas, newly occupied by, the now deceased, Dan. Amlas should be loyal to Vlad and Wallachia, but as they were not actively apprehending and handing over the rebels, Vlad decided to tie up the loose ends himself.

In August of 1460 he rode on Amlas. Once again he burned, looted and killed and demonstrated what happened if you were not with him. He didn't catch Vlad Calugarul, but he must have satisfied himself that he had killed off any rebellion and threat, because he returned to Wallachia to start negotiations with the embassy from Brasov.

The peace treaty was complete by October. It basically restored the original trade agreements and contained agreements on exchange of prisoners and reciprocal payment of damages.

Vlad had now dealt with all his identified enemies and could feel reasonably secure. But there was more to do.

Internal Affairs

Decades of conflict, caused by internal rivalry or warfare, had left Wallachia poor. Peasant would have had their crops stolen or burned and their cattle stolen or confiscated. Multiple armies had been raised, digging deep into the population, which probably only counted around 500,000 at the time of Vlad Dracula. Law and order would have been undermined, beggars and thieves owning the streets.

Theft, fraud, begging and dishonesty in any form became forbidden. As was the case with Vlad's external enemies, defiance meant death, and often in a spectacular fashion as an example to others.

According to legend, Vlad gathered a group of beggars, handicapped and gypsies (all of whom in contemporary opinion probably was one and the same group of 'anti-socials') in Targoviste for a feast, locked the hall and set it on fire, burning all the unwanted elements.

Is it true? Even from a fifteenth century perspective, that would be considered harsh, but then again......

The concentration camps built by the Nazi-regime in Germany 500 years later were initially filled with handicapped, gypsies, homosexuals and other 'unwanted elements' (which included communists and intellectuals critical to the regime). Run as work camps, rather than the purpose built Death Camps that later emerged, these camps aimed to clear the German society from the burden of maintaining people who did not contribute *and* also took care of any political dissidents.

It is thus far from impossible that Vlad Dracula, at a time where human life was worth significantly less than in twentieth Century Germany would have come up with a similar solution to get rid of his unwanted elements, and again set an example for others.

For the population of Wallachia, Vlad's regime meant a period of stability, peace and prosperity. He had cut the Boyars down to size (no doubt winning many common hearts). He had put a stop to major conflict and he had if not eliminated then surely majorly reduced theft, begging, fraud and crime in general.

The legends once again have something to say about this. According them, in Targoviste there was a Golden Cup standing by a communal well. Travellers would wonder how that was possible, but the locals would laugh at them and explained that with Vlad Dracula as Voivode the cup was safe. This is not a new story, it has been told about others before Vlad Tepes, but the fact that it has survived in folklore gives us a good idea of how the common people thought of Vlad; he became a popular hero, a status he has maintained up until today.

If you doubt my words, let us have a quick look at the nineteenth century "Scrisoarea a iii a" poem by poet laureate Mihai Eminescu that I have mentioned previously in the Foreword of this book:

> *'Rise once more, o Tepes ! Take and divide these men,*
> *as lunatics and rogues in two big tribes, and then*
> *in mighty, twin infirmaries by force both tribes intern,*
> *and with a single faggot prison and madhouse burn.'*

The 'infirmaries' burned with 'a single faggot' refer to the legendary burning of the unwanted anti-social element. According to Eminescu, and still taught in Romanian schools in the twenty-first century, that is a good solution that by popular opinion should be repeated on today criminals and other unwanted elements (which would probably include gypsies, still in twenty-first century Romania seen as thieves and beggars by default).

I don't think that Vlad set out to be a hero of the people; I think his reasons were far more pragmatic. First of all he wanted to protect himself, and secondly he needed peace and prosperity to secure against revolt and unrest, as well as he needed men and food for his army, because he was not exactly done yet.

Vlad may well have subscribed to Caligula's favourite quote from Lucius Accius; 'Let them hate me as long as they fear me', but having his people behind him would not have hurt him, even if only as a side effect to his main purposes.

Vlad and the Church

Before we continue the story, let us have a look at Vlad's relation to the Church. This is important because a classic feudal society like the one in Wallachia would have had three basic social classes.

The landowners (Boyars), and the Voivode appointed by them, were top of the pile in all matters physical and practical. They effectively owned the lives and bodies of the second class, the peasants (there were no major cities in Wallachia in Vlad's time and thus no middle class of "citizens").

The third class was the Church, and the priests and monks associated with the Church. Where the landowners owned the bodies of the peasants, The Church owned their souls, and it was important for both the landowners and the Church that the two worked in some kind of unison. To cut it down to the basics, both the landowners and the Church derived their income from the labour of the peasants, and discord between the two was not good for business.

Vlad would have been brought up as an (Greek) Orthodox, and would thus have been of a different religion than both the powerful empires surrounding him, Catholic Hungary and Islamic Ottomans. Of course he would be closer to the Hungarians in this aspect, being of a different Christian denomination rather than a completely different religion, but such matters were important in those days, and still is to some today (look up John F Kennedy and note how he still to this day is referred to as 'the only Catholic President of the Unites States of America').

Historical documents show that Vlad was a frequent donator of money and property to the Church, a classic role of a ruler, not only in Wallachia - but he took it further.

The head of the Wallachian church was the Metropolitan. He was appointed by the Patriarch in Constantinople, and was normally a foreigner. With the fall of Constantinople in 1453 a new power vacuum appears as, even though Mehmed had appointed a new Patriarch (in line with the Ottoman principle of religious freedom and autonomy in their conquered areas), the Orthodox Church was effectively split and without a clear head.

Once again Vlad pounces into the gap, and in 1457 he appointed his own, Wallachian, Metropolitan, the former abbot Iosif. Vlad now has his own pliant head of the Church, and has effectively fused the Church and the State. He is now in control of both the bodies and the souls of his people.

But was Vlad a religious man?

Well, not necessarily. As we have already seen in other cases, there are more than one side to Vlad and so it is too in this aspect.

On the one side are Vlad's laws. His clamping down on thieves, beggars and other anti-social and criminal elements have strong undertones of the Ten Commandments. Even if you were ignorant to the exact laws of the land, if you stuck to the basics of the Ten Commandments, then you would probably also stay reasonably within Vlad's laws.

On the other hand we have a historically documented pragmatism in regards religion. In an agreement between Sultan Mehmed and Vlad Dracula from 1460, one of the points specify that if a Wallachian converted to Islam while in the Ottoman territories, he would revert to the Orthodox faith on his return. In many other places such wavering between religions would be considered heretic and subject to death and damnation, but in Vlad's Wallachia (and Mehmed's Ottoman Empire) pragmatic realism once again prevailed.

One interesting aspect also is that Vlad, despite his good relationship with the Orthodox Church, had little time and patience with Catholic monks. Indeed he made himself an enemy with many such, something that, ironically, would eventually propel him into immortality!

Catholic monks would have filtered over the border from Hungarian Transylvania, both as emissaries and missionaries. Some argue, that Vlad's dislike of them was based on protection of the Orthodox Church against such Catholic intruders, or if he was indeed a deeply religious person (which I doubt as per the above), he would have seen the missionaries as a threat to the very souls of his people. I personally think that his dislike of the monks were two-fold and not rooted in religion at all.

First he would have considered them with a, probably well founded, suspicion in terms of their true purpose and suspected that they were acting as spies for their Hungarian, or in many cases, Saxon masters.

Secondly, in an interestingly pre-Lutheran way of thinking, he would have seen them as a combination of thieves and beggars that would have been in direct opposition to his laws. Catholic monks would notoriously be selling absolution, a key issue for Martin Luther, and if we are to read his reaction, also a key issue with Vlad Dracula.

Whether for one or the other reason, Vlad had several run-ins with Catholic monks and even had some killed, thus creating a new and dangerous group of enemies that could not be eradicated or brought to submission the way he had dealt with his other enemies.

Modernisation

The centre of Wallachian government was in Targoviste, and although there was a royal compound, it was a "Palace" rather than a castle. It had originally been built by Vlad's grandfather, Mircea Cel Batran, and it contained administrative, formal and residential buildings, as well as a church. It was surrounded by a low wall, aimed at holding off a peasant revolt rather than a besieging army. It is today an interesting ruin, but whereas it was Vlad's home, it was not the kind of castle that we would associate with a fifteenth century prince.

The thing is that Wallachia wasn't really well suited for castles. Apart from the mountain-border with Transylvania, Wallachia is rather flat and traditional castles would have had no natural advantages in terms of the surrounding terrain.

The only places suited for castles were strategic border-points, more precisely the border-passes in the Carpathian Mountains in the north and the crossing points on the Danube River in the south.

The border in the north saw important border-crossings in Bran, Poienari and Turnu Rosu and the Danube River saw important crossing-points in Chilia, Giurgiu and Vidin. The Danube castles were however not under Vlad's control.

The castle in Chiliaa, guarding access to the Danube from the Black Sea was, according to agreements leading back to Janos Hunyadi, held by Hungarian troops and the Ottomans presently had control of the castles in Giurgiu and Vidin.

The Wallachian castles were not the power-base castles known from many other parts of Europe. They were first and foremost built as border-posts and customs-points, held by castellans loyal to the Voivode.

Neither were they particularly new, the youngest of them probably being the one at Giurgiu, built by Vlad's grandfather. And therein lay a problem that Vlad decided to do something about.

The problem was that, as imposing and intimidating as they may have looked at their mountain passes or overlooking river crossings, they were in effect becoming obsolete. The issue was that in the decades, or even centuries, between their construction and Vlad's time, military technology had changed dramatically and these castles were not built for modern warfare with cannons.

In 1446, Sultan Mural II used cannons to shatter the Hexamilion wall of the Isthmus of Corinth and his son, the current sultan Mehmed, had demonstrated the devastating effect that cannon had on defensive walls both during the conquest of Constantinople and the Siege of Belgrade.

For centuries castles, and other defensive walls, had been built as solid stone walls. That was sufficient against the, centuries old, technology of hurling big rocks from catapults. The modern balls propelled from cannons were however so powerful that they effectively splintered and cracked the solid walls, creating breaches that attacking infantry could use to penetrate the defences.

The most current technique at the time was to use smaller cannons to hit three spots similar to the end points of a triangle and then hit in the middle of the triangle with a bigger cannon. This technique would take out a complete section of the wall.

The most current method of mobile warfare, as deployed by Mehmed at Belgrade, had cannon cast on the spot, so cannons were becoming the most modern and devastating technology, effectively rendering the formerly powerful castles redundant. And there was a further problem.

In a reaction to the threat of the Ottoman in front of Constantinople, the Byzantine defenders had come up with a plan for how to defend against them. In its simplest form it is still used in twenty-first Century warfare; you fight artillery with you own artillery, and the party with the longest ranging artillery can take out the other party's artillery from a safe distance. With this in mind, the Byzantines deployed their own cannons on the top of their ancient Land Wall. Better protected and with the higher position, these cannon could reach further than the Ottoman cannons, and they should in principle be able to destroy the Ottoman artillery.

When the Byzantine defenders deployed their cannons, it however turned out that they were so powerful in their recoil that the walls underneath them cracked, assisting the attackers rather than the defenders. The problem was the same as for the walls' defensive capabilities; a solid wall had very little flexibility and could not absorb the energy, whether from a cannon ball or from cannon being fired.

The engineering solution was to change the way defensive walls were built, into a design with two walls built in stone or brick (brick in itself being able to absorb energy and not splintering like stone) with a softer (rubble) core between them. In addition walls were made lower and thicker, and where possible square designs were replaced by rounded or, as time went by, triangular designs that represented less of a direct target for cannons.

With this in mind, Vlad started a modernisation project aiming at upgrading the Wallachian castles to modern warfare.

It is unclear exactly how far this programme went, but it most definitely covered a complete renovation of the border-castle in Poienari, the exact project in which he allegedly used Boyars and their families as slave labour, and should you visit Poienari castle today, then you can clearly see how the walls are constructed to withstand cannon fire.

Vlad also decided to modernise the central administration, indeed he started a project to move the capital city. The problem he had with Targoviste was that it was too far away from the border with the Ottomans, the most likely theatre of conflict. Instead he identified a village closer to the Danube, a day's travel north of the important border-crossing at Giurgiu, and there he started to build a new government compound, which he used as his main seat of government from 1459. The name of the village was Bucharest, the capital of modern day Romania.

Secure

Around 1460, Vlad could feel reasonably secure, probably for the first time in his adult life. The Boyars and the Saxons were under control, he ruled with the blessing of both the Hungarians and the Ottomans and his cousin Stefan now ruled in Moldavia.

Law and order prevailed in his land, where he was loved by most and feared by the rest. He had started to modernise his country's defenses and had moved his government to Bucharest.

He had of course previously been in situations that looked relatively good, but where events around him had turned things upside down and spurned his fate along with it. This time, however, it was Vlad who was in control, and there was no immediate danger to the stability and peace he had created.

For all intents and purposes, his strategy of merciless and cruel punishment of anyone who was not with him had paid off. A few had been sacrifices, the many reaped the benefits.

Vlad could have probably ruled Wallachia for many years to come, and could have become one of the few rulers that got to old age and death by natural causes, even if he had created enemies along the way. But it just wasn't in Vlad's nature to rest on his laurels. Whereas the events that turned the World may not have forced his hand this time, there were plenty of things happening that he could choose to be part of, and choose he did.

Sir Jens

CHAPTER 5
AGGRESSOR

Sir Jens

Mathias

While Vlad Dracula was busy consolidating his grip on power in Wallachia, the new king of Hungary, Mathias, was doing exactly the same thing, though by different means.

Mathias, the younger son of Janos Hunyadi, had quickly been put on the Hungarian throne by the Hungarian nobility following the sudden death of the unpopular King Ladislav Posthumous in 1457.

The choice of Mathias was the culmination of an ongoing battle between the Hungarian nobility and what they saw as foreign interference, but their choice of king was not without complications.

In principle it was the Holy Roman Emperor (who in effect was the Emperor of Germany, which wasn't an empire!) who appointed the King of Hungary, based on dynastic bloodlines. Mathias was not of a royal bloodline, indeed his father had only been ennobled in 1409, and Mathias was, albeit noble, in principle not a candidate.

Doctrine was that the King of Hungary had to be crowned with the Crown of St. Stephen, Hungary's ancient royal crown and that was in the physical possession of the Emperor Frederich III, who had no intentions of handing it over.

Indeed the whole business with the Hungarian Diet, the parliament of nobles, just choosing their own king was so novel, and such a break with how things were done, that it sent shockwaves across Europe, and set the young king off to a rather rocky start.

Armed conflict followed, and though the Hungarians managed to fight off both the Roman Emperor and the King of Poland (who took the opportunity to also lay claim to the Hungarian throne), they needed a powerful ally, and as we shall see a little later, that ally became the Pope in Rome.

Before it came to that, Mathias, no doubt eagerly encouraged by his uncle Mihai Szilagy (the same Mihai Szilagy who had gotten Vlad involved in Hungary's internal affairs a few years earlier), put his own stake in the ground. Without consulting with the nobles in the Diet he levied a new tax, and with the money he bought himself a mercenary army and rode on Bosnia.

The background for this is longwinded, and outside the subject of our story, but in essence, Serbia had been thrown into a typical civil war of succession. Mathias took matters in his own hands and went in support of the party favoring unity with Bosnian and Hungary. Though he took position as overlord of both countries, it didn't really make much difference in the end as by the end of 1459, the Ottomans has once again advanced and successfully taken all of Serbia, leaving further bickering and in-fighting obsolete.

Coming back to Mathias and the Pope, it was really a combination of factors that brought them together. The newly elected Pope Pius II was very concerned about the Ottoman expansion and aggression. They might well have suffered a setback at Belgrade, but Pius was convinced that this was not the last to be heard from Mehmed and in an attempt to whip up some real interest he officially called a three year crusade, starting from January 1460.

As had become common practice (as this was not the first call for a crusade against the Ottomans), a number of meetings and conferences took place, and nothing much came of it but talk and empty promises. The Pope promised salvation for all that participated, but it just wasn't enough to get the Christian rulers to commit. The Pope offered money as a further incentive, and a new champion appeared on the otherwise rather empty stage; Mathias of Hungary.

Mathias had three basic priorities. First and foremost he needed peace with his Christian neighbors. Secondly he needed money. Thirdly he needed to settle the issue with the Roman Emperor and get the Crown of St. Stephen back, as in many people's mind he was a usurper without it.

The Pope could provide the first two and ultimately, though indirectly, the third as well.

So Matthias showed a piece of amazing statesmanship, a precursor for what was to come under his rule, and sprang onto the stage as the new Athleta Christi (Defender of Christ), the rallying point for the Pope's crusade and the defense of Christianity itself.

The Pope immediately intervened in Hungary's affairs, and brokered, if not directly demanded, peace between Mathias and his powerful neighbors. The Pope needed Mathias to concentrate on the forthcoming crusade.

Next the Pope gave Mathias large sums of money to build up the Crusader Army. Others had money from the papal coffers too, but it was Mathias who took the lion's share.

Though he still had to get his hands on the Crown of St. Stephen, Mathias had so far gotten two of his three top priorities sorted out by allying himself with the Pope, and the Pope had found himself a champion.

Ottoman Expansion

Though having suffered a setback at Belgrade, Mehmed had no intentions of stopping his expansion. In July 1456, he returned from Belgrade to Edirne, Istanbul still not being the official capital of the Ottoman Empire, though Mehmed had started a range of projects to rebuild and repopulate his great prize.

Even though he had formerly mopped up resistance from the last few fragments of the former Byzantine Empire, he had in line with his polices left them alone, as long as they paid tribute and didn't cause trouble.

The former Byzantine enclave in the Morea, governed by the brothers of the last Byzantine Emperor, had stopped paying tribute, and was engulfed in civil war. Mehmed had enough and personally led an army south through Greece to put a stop to further unrest.

The Morea fell quickly, apart from the city of Corinth itself which was left besieged, and Mehmed took the opportunity to mop up any other pockets of potential resistance in Greece, including conquest of the independent city-state of Athens. He really didn't meet much concerted resistance, and was soon back in Edirne.

In parallel to the campaign in Greece, Mehmed had sent an army to Serbia. Contrary to Bulgaria, which was run as a full Ottoman Pashalik, or Region, without local government, Serbia had remained a vassal state under local government, but paying annual tribute to the Ottomans. With a war of succession at hand, and with Hungary's attempt to take over, Mehmed had decided that it was time to permanently solve the issue of Serbia's loyalty.

The Ottoman army marched, with little resistance through Serbia, took fortress by fortress and finally took its, basically undefended, capital of Smederevo in June 1459.

With the Ottomans now in possession of Serbia, the Hungarians and Ottomans started years of mutual cross-border raiding, the avoidance of which was the exact reason for Wallachia's existence as a buffer-zone.

Next in line in Mehmed's expansion politics was the Empire of Trebizond, the last remaining part of the former Byzantine Empire, which despite the impressive name was reduced to a small city-state on the Black Sea coast. A campaign in 1461 saw the relative easy defeat of Trebizond, which was the last nail in the coffin of the Byzantine Empire.

Crusader

At the time the Hungarians and Ottomans fought it out over Serbia, Vlad was finishing up his own mopping up of any potential threats and was in a relatively secure position.

His safety in regards to the Ottomans, however, came at a price. He had to keep paying the annual tribute in gold and boys that had long been established and renewed under the rule of his father. Up until, and including, 1459 Vlad paid the tribute and peace was secured.

I have mentioned earlier that Vlad made a new agreement with Mehmed in 1460, and according to this agreement the annual tribute should now be paid in Wallachia (rather than being brought to the Ottomans as had been custom before), and the Ottoman embassy should be secured free passage to Targoviste and back to the border crossing at Giurgiu, where a receipt would be issued and matters settled.

This gesture shows that the Ottomans were quite happy to give small concessions as long as peace was maintained, but it turned out to be a waste of their time and effort.

Despite his feeling of relative security, Vlad was not a man to sit down and wait for disaster to strike. He had seen it happen often enough and had enjoyed success with his more direct approach of striking proactively at potential danger, and Vlad now saw danger coming from the Ottomans.

There is no single explanation as to why Vlad in 1460 decided to stop paying the tributes and stir up the relationship with the Ottomans, but his reasons shall probably once again be seen on the basis of a wider view.

We have previously covered the fact that Wallachia had avoided outright annexation through its position as a convenient buffer between the Hungarian and Ottoman empires. One of Vlad's possible problems was that the same could be said about Serbia, which contrary to Bulgaria, had not been fully annexed by the Ottomans, as that also would have meant a direct border between the Hungarians and the Ottomans. This however was no longer true.

With the Ottoman annexation of Serbia in 1459, Mehmed had displayed a clear defiance for the problems a direct border with Hungary would cause. Indeed he had quite happily engaged in a ping-pong game of reciprocal border-raids, which saw his troops making raids into Hungary and Bosnia and Hungarian troops making raids into Serbia.

One such Hungarian raid, in 1460, was led by Vlad's ally and supporter, and the uncle to King Mathias, Mihai Szilagy. The raiders were captured and the troops beheaded while Mihai himself was subjected to three days of torture in order to provide information about Hungary and subsequently killed, according to legend by being sawed in halves. Vlad Dracula had plenty of inspiration for his more spectacular methods of killing his enemies.

If we try to see this from the perspective of Vlad, then Mehmed's new approach to sharing borders with Hungary suddenly undermined the core reason for Wallachia's existence.

After Mehmed's unsuccessful attempt at taking Belgrade, and thus opening the door to Hungary and Western Europe, it was not unreasonable to conclude that he had changed strategy and would quite happily start building up an extended border with Hungary in preparation for his next attempt. Indeed, this would spread the potential points of attack out, and not make his target as easily predictable as Belgrade had been. If his annexation of Serbia was anything to judge from, then Wallachia,

Bosnia and Moldavia were the very likely candidates for the next annexations.

Mathias, now suffering Ottoman raids into Hungary itself, had also taken notice of this new strategy and some believe that his counter-move was to ask Vlad to start his own raids into Bulgaria in order to spread out the Ottoman troops (and rather cynically let the Ottoman revenge-raids go into Wallachia rather than Hungary proper). He would have promised Vlad support when that time came.

On this basis Vlad made a deliberate decision to take on the Ottomans. And as we shall soon see, stopping the tributes was only the first stage in an escalating aggression.

The Ottomans first tried to sort things out through diplomacy; they sent letters and even an embassy, to Vlad, reminding him of his obligations.

There is some doubt about Vlad's exact reaction. Legend has one version, and other sources have another.

According to legend, Vlad had the turbans of the visiting Ottoman ambassadors nailed to their heads, with the excuse that they had refused to take them off in his presence.

Ottoman sources says that Vlad responded (which implies that the ambassadors lived to bring back an answer), that he had no money left after his warfare in Transylvania. In either case, the answer was 'no'.

The Ottomans tried again, but this time there was a sting in the tail to their apparent desire to sort things out peacefully.

In late 1461 they sent a new embassy to Vlad, or rather halfway, namely to the (Ottoman controlled) border-crossing at Giurgiu. The embassy was led by Hamsa Bey, who had successfully commanded the Ottoman fleet during the conquest of Constantinople and now commanded the crossing point at Vidin on the Danube. With him was

Thomas Catavolenus, Mehmed's Private Secretary. This high-level embassy now invited Vlad to come to Giurgiu and talk things over, but their motives were not as honest as they seemed.

Mehmed must have sensed that Vlad Dracula was becoming a real problem, enough of a problem that he wanted him apprehended and brought to him Edirne.

One can only speculate that Vlad's appearance in Edirne would in the best case have led to a humiliating peace-agreement (as was the case when his own father had come to the sultan in 1443 and had been forced to leave Vlad and his brother, Radu, behind as hostages) and in the worst case have led to his death, not unlikely by his own preferred method of terror-killing; impalement.

How Vlad became aware of this direct threat to his life is unknown, perhaps his survival instinct was just so well developed by now that he took the necessary precautions in any case, but the planned ambush on Vlad Dracula went terribly wrong, and it was the Ottoman troops who were ambushed. The common troops were killed, and Hamsa Bey and Thomas Catavolenus were carried off as prisoners.

This turn of events would not have pleased Mehmed, who would have personally sanctioned the mission, but the situation could probably still have been resolved even at this extended stage of aggression as, at the end of the day, both Vlad and Mehmed had transgressed and some kind of peace could most likely be found, including the safe return of the two captured dignitaries. But Vlad had no intentions of peace and indeed he came prepared for further provocation.

Having ambushed the ambush and captured the would-be captors, Vlad moved on. He had brought with him a troop of Wallachian cavalry in Ottoman uniforms (or perhaps they just used the uniforms of the executed

Ottoman troops). They were capable of speaking sufficient Turkish to make the Ottoman troops in the castle in Giurgiu think they were their own troops, so the gates were opened and Vlad's troops took the castle, executed the Ottoman garrison and burned the castle. And that was not all, far from it, Vlad was just warming up.

Having secured the border-crossing Vlad and his marauders continued into Bulgaria and for 2 weeks they rode along the Danube and indiscriminately killed anyone they considered to be allied with the Ottomans. They destroyed several border fortifications and crossing points, and though they killed many of their enemies, they also took many prisoners, civilians and soldiers alike, who were marched off to Targoviste and later would play an infamous role in the story of Vlad Dracula.

Among all the folklore, this raid is well documented, by no less than Vlad himself. He wrote to King Mathias, giving him a detailed description of the places he had attacked, and the thousands (probably exaggerated) of enemies he had killed.

To make sure the message was clear it starts '*So that you know Your Highness, that I broke peace with them [the Ottomans] not for any use of ours, but to honour you, Your Highness, and for the sake of the Sacred Crown of Yours, and for keeping Christianity as a whole, and unifying the Catholic law*'.

Vlad specifically makes a point of the fact that he has destroyed all the crossing-points except the one at Vidin.

He then asks that Mathias send his whole army to Wallachia (preferably by April the following year), or that he at least sends troops and arms from Transylvania, because '*As soon as the weather gets better, that is, in spring, they are going to come back as enemies, with all their strength*'.

In other words, Vlad went into this act of war with his eyes wide open, and he was well aware that there was no more room for peace and that Mehmed would come at him. No more letters, no more embassies and no more skulduggery. The relatively small issue of Vlad's tribute had now, and very much by Vlad's own doing, escalated into full scale war.

Before we move on, we need to have a look at what Vlad actually thought would happen next. As he was fully aware of his actions, and the reaction they would demand, he must have had some kind of plan in mind.

It is highly unlikely that Vlad, despite his fine words on the defence of Christianity (and Catholic law), had suddenly turned crusader, even though he admittedly was the only Christian ruler who did much over and above talking and taking the Pope's money. Vlad was a realist, and he would have not thought that taking on Mehmed entirely on his own was an attractive proposition.

So he must have thought that he could count on Hungary, or at least their forces in Transylvania, to boost his own relatively small army, and he had some justification for thinking so.

Mathias had, as previously covered, emerged as the front figure of the crusade called by Pope Pius II, and he had readily used the Pope to broker peace and provide him with money, supposedly to build up an army with which to fight the Ottomans. Furthermore, as mentioned, it is very possible that Mathias had proactively urged Vlad on to raid into Ottoman Bulgaria.

But Vlad had misread Mathias' immediate priorities. Yes Mathias wanted peace with his neighbours, and yes he wanted money, both of which had been supplied by the Pope, but his remaining priority at that time was not a full scale war with the Ottomans, it was the Crown of St. Stephen and with that his legitimacy as king.

As long as Mathias had not been properly crowned, he was in essence a usurper and he could not ensure lasting peace, internally or externally. Indeed he would probably have feared that should he lead an army towards the Ottomans, then he may well leave the door open for a coup in his absence. He had some cause for this concern as exiled dissidents had already once attempted to crown Emperor Frederich as King of Hungary (in absentia) in 1459.

If Vlad had provoked an Ottoman expedition force to come to Wallachia, then Mathias would have probably been happy to lend some assistance, but he was simply not prepared for a full-on battle with the Ottomans at this time, and rather than look at Vlad as a brave crusader, creating a perfect opportunity for Mathias to take on Mehmed, he would have probably seen him as a loose cannon, whose actions were at best inconvenient, at worst catastrophic. Mathias wasn't coming to meet the full Ottoman army in Wallachia and Vlad was on his own.

Indeed, in the whole of Mathias' reign, which lasted until 1490, he never went into a full scale battle with the Ottomans. He fought many skirmishes and battled it out for strategic castles as well as he raided into Ottoman held territories, but not on a single occasion did he commit the full Hungarian army into a pitched battle with the Ottomans. Indeed his military achievements were mainly aimed at other Christian rulers, in particular in a fight for Bohemia and Austria (which he partly annexed into Hungary),

As a by-line, Mathias managed to finally get his hands on The Crown of St. Stephen by using a large part of the money he got from the Pope to buy the crown from the Emperor (for 60,000 ducats), and get himself properly crowned (this time by the grace of God, rather than only the Hungarian Diet) in 1464.

Alone

Vlad's raid on the Ottoman possessions along the Danube in the winter of 1461 became legendary. The Pope himself, followed by a range of European rulers expressed their pleasure and gratitude and the Knights of Rhodes had Te Deums song in his praise.

Vlad had become a crusader hero, except with Mathias, who was the only one who could actually help him with what he needed in lieu of praise and Te Deums; soldiers.

His friend Stefan of Moldavia could not help him either. He had his own troubles, balancing precariously between loyalty to Hungary and Poland, a balance that was gradually turning into full scale conflict with Hungary. Indeed an issue of contention between Stefan and Vlad was the contingent of Hungarian troops who (since an agreement dating back to 1448) held the castle at Chilia on the border between Wallachia and Moldavia, something he would take the opportunity to sort out soonest.

So Vlad had to fall back on Plan B; meeting Mehmed's army in Wallachia. Even though this was clearly not what he had hoped for, he must have considered the option that it could be the end result, and he had some room for cautious optimism.

As I have mentioned before, there would have been plenty of stories told in Wallachia about Vlad's grand-father Mircea Cel Batran's defense against the Ottomans in 1394, where guerilla tactics and a clever choice of terrain had seen of Sultan Bayzid's otherwise superior army. Those stories may well have forgotten the fact that though militarily successful, Mircea in the end had to flee Wallachia and later stage a Hungarian backed coup to regain the throne from the Ottoman backed Voivode.

Similarly inspirational, and also covered earlier, was Skanderbeg's contemporary defense of Albania, which still caused Mehmed headaches and constant trouble at the western end of his Empire.

I have earlier speculated that Vlad would have taken the opportunity during his somewhat idle interregnum years to learn the art of guerilla warfare from Skanderbeg, but whether he did or not, he would soon show that somehow he had picked it up to near perfection. Not that he had much choice, Mehmed was coming and Vlad was abandoned and left alone in the defense of Wallachia, albeit with lots of moral support he could use for nothing.

As expected, Mehmed could not leave Vlad's provocation unanswered indeed he is reported to have been so angry that he personally beat the messenger who brought him news of Vlad's attack. He already had Skanderbeg causing trouble in the west and the 'Lord of the White Sheep', Uzun Hasan, the Turkmen ruler of Eastern Anatolia, causing trouble in the east (there were even rumors of an alliance between Uzun Hasan and the Pope), and he had plenty of other small principalities (including Moldavia) paying tribute, so he had to make an example of what happened if you negated on your agreement.

Having already attempted to catch and deal with Vlad in isolation, he had no choice but to march on Wallachia and as there were no other major engagements planned, he came in person and with the full force of the Ottoman army.

With the Ottoman army came also Vlad's younger brother Radu, who had opted to stay with the Ottomans after his father's death in 1447.

Mehmed is well known to have been, if not outright homosexual then, distinctly bi-sexual and Ottoman chronicles specifically mention that Radu, who would later be known as "Cel Frumos" (The Beautiful) for his good looks, caught young Mehmed's eye and, after initial resistance, showed himself amendable to Mehmed's advances.

It was however not in this capacity that Radu accompanied Mehmed's army as Mehmed's preference was young boys, and Radu would be close on 30 years old at the time. Radu was Mehmed's choice of successor to the Wallachian throne, once he had dealt with Vlad, should he decide to not annex Wallachia completely.

The first obstacle faced by the Ottoman army was crossing the Danube. In a strategic move during his winter raids, Vlad had destroyed most of the crossing-points, but he had left Vidin intact and it was predictably here the Ottoman army first tried to cross the river.

The details are sparse, but an eye-witness account exists, even though it is not exactly reliable in its details. From this we can gather that Vlad's first line of defense was the river itself and that he initially managed to repel the Ottoman crossing. The Ottoman army, however, spread out, and crossed the river by boat to build a small bridgehead further down the river. When Vlad became aware of this he attacked, but the Ottoman bridgehead had become too strong, and after a bloody skirmish the Ottomans prevailed and Vlad withdrew. What was to follow was classic guerilla warfare, assisted by an unpredictable ally; the weather.

The summer of 1462 was unusually warm. Indeed it was so warm that the eyewitness account says you could cook kebabs on the soldier's mail-shirts. This was in favor of Vlad's plan as the first element of his strategy was to keep the Ottoman army without supplies, in particular food and water. To do so Vlad burned the ground behind him.

The large Ottoman army relied on food and water found on the way, and scouts constantly rode ahead of the main army to find fresh supplies. But wherever they looked the found the same picture, burned fields, villages devoid of man or beast and water sources poisoned or filled in with dead animals.

Mehmed was less than impressed with this situation and he alternately blamed the scouts and his commanders for lack of planning. This later indicates that the Ottoman army initially had made no plans for supplies to be brought up from the rear, but was entirely relying on finding local supplies, which they didn't.

While the Ottoman army slowly made its way north through Wallachia, worse for wear after each day of marching, Vlad deployed classic guerilla principles of raiding. The Wallachian cavalry would appear out from the forest, attack and withdraw. Typically they would attack smaller and weaker elements of the Ottoman troops, constantly snapping at Mehmed's heels and forcing the Ottoman army to keep alert at all times.

The Ottomans had one military success though, and ironically it was caused by Stefan of Moldavia, Vlad's supposed friend and ally.

As I have briefly mentioned, Stefan, in escalating conflict with Hungary, was unhappy that the castle at Chilia, on the border of Moldavia, was manned by Hungarian troops. With everybody's eyes on Vlad, Mehmed and Mathias, Stefan took the opportunity to attack the castle at Chilia.

The attempt was unsuccessful, and Stefan himself was wounded in the attempt, but Vlad diverted part of his force (according to the available sources 7,000, but it was probably substantially less) to protect the castle. The Ottomans had also gotten news of the attack and managed to beat Vlad's troops to Chilia and wipe them out in an ambush even though the castle itself remained in Hungarian hands.

The game, however, was never really about numbers, with or without the troops lost at Chilia, Vlad could never hope to beat the Ottoman army in open battle, not even if he deployed the same choice of terrain for a battle that his grand-father had successfully done, and which in turn was a strategy inherited from Alexander the Great and the Battle of Issus.

But there was one more strategic move that Alexander had deployed at Issus, and whether Vlad knew this or not, deliberately or by chance he too decided on that very strategy.

Alexander had realized that the Persian army had one weak point; its command structure completely depended on the King's presence and initiative. Without the King, the army would simply not be able to move, so if the King could be removed, the army would be defeated. Alexander himself led a suicidal cavalry attack straight through the Persian centre and got so close to King Darius III that his spear killed the King's chariot-driver. Even if it didn't kill the king, it was enough to make him flee, and as predicted the Persian army fell apart once he was gone.

Vlad had similarly realised that he could paralyse, and most probably make the Ottoman army turn, if he could kill Mehmed, perhaps even if he could just wound or scare him.

He had good reason to think so, as the command structure in the Ottoman army was not dissimilar to that of the Persian army. Furthermore he would have known that the Ottoman army's flight from Belgrade was partly caused by the fact that Mehmed had been wounded, rendered unconscious and unable to restore order when the army broke (despite, before being wounded, he was hacking with his sword at his own fleeing troops).

So Vlad planned to do like Alexander and personally lead an attack aimed directly at the person of the Sultan. Contrary to Alexander, Vlad didn't have an open battle to use as a launch-pad for the attack, and an attack on the main Ottoman army during the day would be ritual suicide, so Vlad came up with a different idea; a night attack.

The Ottoman camp was a large affair with the sultan's tent in the middle, unmistakable, but heavily protected by janissaries and possibly even a 'wagenburg' of wagons mounted with firearms.

That the attack was daring is an understatement, but fortune favors the bold, and Vlad was closer to changing World history than anybody else who ever took on Mehmed.

Vlad probably deployed the same strategy he had deployed the year before at Giurgiu, disguising his cavalry in Ottoman uniforms, allowing the raiders to ride straight through the Ottoman camp.

Even though one thing is certain, namely that Vlad's attack didn't manage to kill or wound the Sultan; there are two very different versions as to the success of the raid.

The Wallachian version says that the raid was so fast and furious that the Wallachians withdrew (albeit without their main purpose achieved) without the loss of a single man. It furthermore says that Mehmed was so scared that he fled and had to be convinced, practically forced, to return.

The Ottoman version describes the attack as a complete and utter fiasco, with the Wallachians aiming towards the centre of the camp because they thought it was the way out and Vlad's raiders being cut down, even by ten year old boys.

Neither version is, of course, true. The likely truth lies somewhere in the middle, most probably that Vlad's raiders were discovered when they came closer to the well protected middle and a fierce battle broke out between the raiders and the Janissaries in the immediate vicinity of Mehmed's tent. Both sides would have taken loses, but the Sultan was unhurt.

Vlad's desperate attempts at getting the Ottoman army to turn around, which now seems to have been his main military objective, had failed, but he had one more idea to undermine the Ottoman morale and make them realise the futility of their undertaking.

Slowly, and looking over their shoulders day and night, the Ottoman army marched on towards Targoviste, which they expected to be defended. Once they reached the city they, however, found that it was abandoned and undefended.

No doubt wondering what Vlad's next move was, or even silently hoping that he had perhaps just given up and fled, they continued past the city, and there they discovered what exactly he had prepared for them.

What lay in front of the Ottoman army was 'a forest' of impaled bodies. The number of impalements is unknown, as the contemporary sources cannot be trusted when it comes to numbers, but there must have been plenty to make a strong statement, possibly hundreds.

Vlad had basically gotten rid of all the prisoners he had collected in Targoviste, some from the winter's raids into Bulgaria, some from the current campaign and most prominently amongst them Hamsa Bey, captured at Giurgiu after his own failed attempt at capturing Vlad.

The sight must have been terrifying, the stench unbearable and the sheer brutality unbelievable. The moniker "Tepes'" (The Impaler) was born here, and was to become the common name for Vlad Dracula amongst the Ottomans forthwith.

Finally Mehmed had had enough. He had basically achieved his objectives. There was no armed resistance of note left, Targoviste was his and Vlad had obviously fled. He saw to it that Radu was elected Voivode (there was probably a small retinue of exiled Boyars who could make up a make-shift council), left a contingent of troops and turned around to go back to Istanbul (to which he had recently moved the Ottoman court). He was totally exhausted and utterly disgusted.

What had started as a power-demonstration in submission had turned into a messy brawl, nearly cost him his life and shown his army as being vulnerable if opposed by a determined enemy, even it that enemy had a significant numerical disadvantage.

The Wallachian Boyars would have gradually trickled back, some from exile and some with hat in hand, accepting Radu as the new Voivode. Enough was enough, and nobody had any more appetite for war.

But Vlad had not fled Wallachia. Indeed he had holed up in his newly modernised castle in Poienari. This castle was the only Wallachian castle actually placed high above the surrounding terrain, on a lonely rock formation overlooking the road between Wallachia and Fagaras.

Radu sent troops north to get rid of Vlad whom he did not need to have lurking around in the background as a potential rallying point for dissidents. As had now become custom they set up cannons and tried to shoot the castle walls down. But the castle had, as previously mentioned, been modernised with walls designed to withstand cannons, and the locals, loyal to Vlad, made sure that the castle was supplied with food via the numerous mountain and forest tracks known to them, but not to the besiegers.

Vlad's refuge in Poienari is not mentioned in Ottoman sources at all, but folklore exists. According to such, Vlad had brought his (unnamed) wife with him to Poienari, and when it became clear that sooner or later the Ottomans would smoke them out, she decided that she would rather die than be taken prisoner, so she threw herself in the river beneath the castle, which henceforth was known as "the River of the Princess".

Probably still hoping that King Mathias would come to his rescue, Vlad stayed in Poienari for a few weeks, but finally sneaked out over night and rode north into Transylvania, where he continued to the town of Brasov.

In an ironic twist he had come full circle as he was given quarters on Timpa Hill, the very place he had raided and burned when he came for his rival, Dan, in 1459. Here he waited for King Mathias, who had eventually put an army in the field and slowly marched it down through Transylvania.

Vlad would have probably thought that with Mathias' army arriving, albeit late, and Radu left in Wallachia with only a small contingent of Ottoman troops all was not lost. A determined attack could surely restore his rule, and it was unlikely that Mehmed would come back to Wallachia anytime soon.

In theory he was right, but things should turn out very differently and it should be fourteen years until Vlad once again ruled Wallachia.

CHAPTER 6
TRAITOR

Sir Jens

The Waiting Game

When Vlad sat in Brasov in 1462, waiting for the arrival of King Mathias and his army, he would have thought that things were going reasonably well.

First prize would of course have been that Mehmed's army had been beaten and sent packing, but given the circumstances, first and foremost the fact that he had faced the Ottoman army on his own, he had done quite well.

His fear had been that Mehmed was going to turn Wallachia into a full Ottoman Pashalik, but as it had turned out, Mehmed had satisfied himself with replacing Vlad with his younger brother Radu, had turned his army round and only left a small contingent of troops to keep Radu safe.

There can be little doubt that Vlad would have seen this as a success, and would have felt that his cruel wholesale slaughter of prisoners was vindicated by the fact that he had made Mehmed loose heart and go back home.

All that needed to be done now was to send an army, or at least a reasonably sized expedition force, back into Wallachia, defeat or dispel the remaining Ottoman troops, oust Radu, and put Vlad back on the throne, job done!

And he was not alone in this view. As I have mentioned earlier, the Christian world, from the Pope to the Knight's of Rhodes, sang his praises. Vlad's methods may not have been exactly elegant, but mostly he killed infidels, or their sympathisers, and contrary to most everybody else he at least did something. For all intents and purposes, his mini-war with Mehmed was the only real event of the Pope's nearly two years old crusade.

King Mathias, however, had a very different view of the situation.

Letters sent from the Venetian ambassador to the Hungarian court explain that Mathias' concern was not

Wallachia per se, but rather that Mehmed, once finished in Wallachia, would take the opportunity of having his army in the field and once again march on Belgrade.

Sure, it was not in Mathias' interest that Wallachia was turned into a Pashalik, as had happened to Serbia recently, but he apparently didn't see this as the most threatening scenario and he now showed a character-trait that would define him also in the years to come; he waited.

In effect what he did was raise the army and set out to shadow Mehmed. He marched it south through Transylvania and halted it at Sibiu. From here he could strike south-east into Wallachia if necessary or he could march it south-west towards Belgrade if Mehmed's army swung round in that direction.

As it happened, Mehmed didn't annex Wallachia, and having turned his army round, he went home to Istanbul, exhausted and disgusted at the campaign in Wallachia. So with Mehmed taking the ball home, Mathias did what he did best; nothing.

It was only in November that Mathias, having ensured himself that Mehmed's army was indeed going back home, arrived in Brasov and met with Vlad.

Vlad would have been well impatient by now, seeing the opportunity for a quick campaign into Wallachia slip away with the onset of winter. Their meeting in Brasov could well have looked like the scene in the movie "Gladiator" where the crown-prince, Commodus, greets his father, Emperor Marcus Aurelius with the words 'did I miss the battle?' to which Marcus Aurelius ironically answers 'no, you missed the war'.

But despite Vlad's hope for assistance from Mathias, and a quick reversal of his luck, Mathias had already made up his mind in a very different way.

Letters

In early November 1462, at around the same time Mathias finally made his way to Brasov to meet with Vlad, three letters emerged, allegedly, and conveniently, intercepted on their way to the intended recipients.

They were addressed to Sultan Mehmed, his Grand Vizier; Mahmud Pasha and Stefan of Moldavia and they were all signed by Vlad Dracula.

In those letters Vlad propose anti-Hungarian alliances (it is worth remembering the Stefan at that time was hostile to Hungary), to the extent that he offers to kidnap Mathias.

After initial talks between Mathias and Vlad (in which Mathias no doubt would have had some problems explaining his inaction), Mathias sent one of his senior officers, Jan Jiskra, to arrest Vlad. The reason was treason, based on the letters mentioned above.

That the letters were forgeries and most certainly not written by Vlad is an accepted historical view. The spelling is bad and the phrasing out of line with Vlad's normal writing style (for instance he refers to Mehmed as 'Lord and Master'). Over and above this, the proposition is laughable. Vlad still believed in Hungarian support, and even if he didn't he could not in his wildest fantasy have thought that Mehmed would trust him as far as he could throw him. Add the convenient interception of all three letters, which would have been sent by three different couriers should they be real.

So where did the letters come from? Some historians believe they can trace the writer to a monk connected to the Black Church in Brasov, an individual named Johann Reudell, who may have written them as an act of revenge given Vlad's burning of the Church of St. Bartholomew some years before, over and above which, of course, Vlad was a known adversary of Catholic monks in general.

Whether Johann Reudell did write the letters or not, petty revenge was probably not the motive, there were far better ones around.

Another possible scenario is that the letters were written on the instruction of the city-fathers of Brasov, who despite receiving Vlad kindly (assuming he was in with King Mathias and may well be back ruling Wallachia soon) had their own scores to settle with Vlad, who had raided Brasov a few years before and killed plenty of their own. Also, if he was likely to throw Wallachia into further wars, they may not enjoy a stable environment in which to trade. Again this is a possibility, but not the most likely.

The most likely scenario is that the letters were written under instructions of Mathias himself or at least his advisors should the King want deniability (yes; some things never change).

Mathias was facing a crucial dilemma. On one hand he had a nice little scheme going, in which he put up a token effort (without actually getting anywhere close to the enemy), took the Pope's money and was saving to buy his own legitimacy as King of Hungary through possession of the Crown of St. Stephen.

On the other hand he had Vlad Dracula, crusader-hero, the man who got results, loved by the Pope, and bent on taking war (and Mathias' army) to the Ottomans.

Those two scenarios did not fit together, so one had to go. The cost of going to war with Mehmed would strip him of any chance of buying the coveted crown from Emperor Frederich, so the decision was easy; it was Vlad who had to go.

But with Vlad's reputation, and the eyes of the Christian world watching, Mathias couldn't just ignore Vlad, or silence him indiscriminately, he needed a reason, and as has been the case many times throughout history, accusations of treason were the answer. So, instigated by himself or otherwise, Mathias accepted that the letters were genuine and had Vlad arrested.

Needless to say that there was no expedition force being sent to Wallachia where, until further notice, Radu ruled and Mehmed called the shots.

In an isolated incident, and just mentioned for comparison, at the same time Mathias had Vlad arrested, Mehmed dealt with David Comnenus, the former Emperor of Trebizond. After Mehmed's conquest of Trebizond (the year before he went after Vlad in Wallachia), the former emperor had been allowed his freedom and was living in some comfort, probably in or around Edirne. Mehmed, however, had a short memory when it came to promises made to anyone who could potentially cause him competition or stir up revolt, so letters were intercepted in which David allegedly wrote Uzun Hasan (the ruler of Eastern Anatolia) and proposed a union against Mehmed and a resurrection of his former Empire. The letter was false, but it was enough for David, and most of his family, to be executed.

Prisoner

If Vlad had been most anybody else, he too would have been executed, possibly cruelly, but even with accusations of treason and betrayal hanging over him, Vlad was just too much of a favorite with, in particular, the Pope, so he was 'detained' rather than kept under lock and key per se.

The details are sketchy, but seem to follow a route to Hungary via Alba Iulia in Transylvania to Visegrad north of the Hungarian capital of Buda (which at that time was separated from the city of Pest on the opposite side of the Danube River).

Visegrad's old castle was used to house high-level prisoners, commonly in the Solomon Tower, but Vlad was kept in some comfort in the castle itself, probably in private apartments, with serving staff and other trappings of his royal heritage, but a prisoner nevertheless.

And though he was later allowed nominal freedom, as long as he didn't stray or got involved in politics, and moved to a house in Pest, he was a de-facto prisoner for the next thirteen years.

And one wonders what Vlad would have done to pass time during thirteen years of comfortable, but nevertheless, captivity.

He was celebrity, though as we shall see in the next chapter he had somewhat gone from famous to infamous. In that capacity he would have played a role as "entertainment" at the Hungarian court, being presented to visiting dignitaries who would by now have known of his exploits, good or bad. He would have probably also had opportunity to swap war stories with visitors and his advice may even have been taken on military matters.

There is one story, folklore as it is, about Vlad during his time in Pest. According to this, the local constables were chasing a thief, and as the thief went through Vlad's property so did the constables. Vlad himself should have appeared with his sword and killed the leading constable with the argument (when he was later questioned by the King) that the constable had essentially committed suicide when he deliberately invaded the domains of a Prince.

Another story, this time written by a Russian traveler referring to what he has heard (rather than seen), says that Vlad would kill mice and birds and impale them on sticks.

I shall leave it with you, the reader, to make up your own mind on such matters.

He also got married to Ilona Szilagy, a cousin of King Mathias, in connection with which he may have converted to Catholicism, something we have already seen he would have considered a purely political move, which could be reverted as and when required. There is speculation that he, like his father before him, was invested in the Order of the Dragon, but that is exactly that, speculation.

My personal opinion is that Vlad first and foremost would have been bored, very bored, and would have taken every opportunity to whisper in King Mathias' ear that it was never too late for him to return to Wallachia and fight the King's enemies. Eventually he would get his way, but we once again need to look beyond Vlad's isolated captivity to follow the bigger events that led to that.

King at Last

Bosnia had long been attempting to play it down the middle, pressured by Hungary, the Ottomans and the Venetians, who held long, narrow parts of the Bosnian coastline.

Mathias' intervention in 1458 meant that Bosnia nominally was under Hungary's protection, currently ruled by Stjepan Tomasevic, but all was far from well.

The Ottoman annexation of Serbia (also nominally protected by Hungary) in 1459 meant that Bosnia, like Wallachia, and Moldavia, was a very likely target for Mehmed's new strategy of expansion up to the borders of Hungary itself (Croatia, with the exception of the city-state of Dubrovnik and Venetian enclaves on the coast, being part of Hungary).

After his return from Wallachia, and having overseen an expedition to the island of Lesbos in the Aegean Sea (where he had 300 Italian prisoners sawed in half), Mehmed got serious about Bosnia.

The first sign that Mehmed was planning something was that he, on his return from Wallachia, instituted a strict regime on correspondence leaving his Empire. From personal communication over trade-letters to diplomatic post, a strict censorship was imposed to ensure that no knowledge of his military dispositions left the Empire. To break the rules was punished by death.

Secondly he started to confiscate goods useable for warfare, such as metal and leather, from foreign traders on Ottoman soil. Needless to say that resistance meant sudden death.

Thirdly he emulated his own method of sealing off access to Constantinople from the Black Sea by building two new fortresses opposite each other, this time further south at the Dardanelles and the entrance to the Mediterranean Sea, now completely controlling naval access to the Sea of Marmara and his new capital of Istanbul.

Fourthly he established new shipyards in Istanbul and in the Dardanelles and started building ships by the hundreds, the Ottomans only now starting to catch up with the Christian countries, and in particular the Italian city-states, in terms of naval capacity and technology.

Mehmed was yet again ready for war, both defensively and offensively, and even when in the spring of 1463 he starting leading his army out of Istanbul, it marched without specific orders to avoid anyone giving away his intentions. Despite leading his army off the direct route his target was, however, not that difficult to guess; he was going to Bosnia.

The Ottoman army subdued Bosnia without too much trouble, executing the King despite having given him letters of safe passage and Mehmed then went into Herzegovina with an expedition force. The terrain there was mountainous and the locals, like Skanderbeg and Vlad Dracula before them, were experts in guerilla warfare. They harassed Mehmed's army, which mainly consisted of cavalry, so intensely that they eventually gave up and turned around. Memories of the preceding year's unhappy campaign in Wallachia against Vlad Dracula no doubt fresh in their minds.

Finally Mehmed installed his own governor in Bosnia, which, like Serbia before it, had now been turned into an Ottoman Pashalik.

The Ottoman annexation of Bosnia was the last straw that finally (no doubt helped along by the Pope) saw Emperor Frederich realise that he had to make peace with King Mathias, as Christian in-fighting would see Mehmed eventually breaking through the thin barrier left between him and Western Europe proper.

A prize for the Crown of St. Stephen was set and paid, and once this was done Mathias was finally ready to move. He went to Bosnia and though he didn't manage to fully retake it, he managed to take control of the strategically important fortress at Jajce, which despite several attempts by the Ottomans, remained in Hungarian hands.

The Ottomans and the Hungarians alternating would try to regain full control of Bosnia over the next six decades, but that is outside the scope of this story.

As it was, Mathias was seen as victorious for the time being and under great pomp and circumstance finally crowned with the Crown of St. Stephen in Buda in 1464. Vlad would have been present at the coronation, as he had been present during the coronation of King Vladislav only twelve years prior. At that time he had been in the company of Mathias' father, Janos Hunyadi, this time he was on his own.

Moldavian Intervention

Vlad's cousin Stefan of Moldavia had, as mentioned, taken a confrontational stand to Hungary and once again had his eyes on the fortress at Chilia, a fortress that controlled access to the Danube from the Black Sea and which, together with the fortress at Akkerman secured the south-eastern part of Moldavia and thus Moldavia's access to the Black Sea itself.

His attempt in 1462, parallel to the Ottoman offensive against Vlad, had not given him what he wanted (indeed had been shot in the foot in the attempt), so in 1465 he came again. This time he succeeded to beat the Hungarian garrison and take control of the fortress.

Mathias now had enough of Stefan's anti-Hungarian policies and went against him in order to secure a more pliant ruler. The armies met in battle outside Baia in the winter of 1467.

The Hungarians were beaten - Mathias himself wounded thrice by arrows (in the back) and, according to a contemporary source 'carried from the battlefield on a stretcher, to avoid him falling into the hands of the enemy'. Stefan had secured his western border and eliminated the immediate risk of subjection to Hungary, but he was far from safe.

In a separate note, on their way to the battle of Baia the Hungarian army went through the town of Roman. There, according to contemporary sources, they killed the population indiscriminately 'without considering their sex, age, or looks'.

Stefan and Mathias were not the only contenders for the fortress at Chilia, or for that matter the control of Moldavia itself, Mehmed had his own plans.

With Wallachia for the time being under the control of Vlad's brother, Radu Cel Frumos, who was fiercely loyal to Mehmed, and with Serbia and (most parts of) Bosnia annexed into the Ottoman Empire, the last remaining buffer-state between the Ottomans and the Hungarians was Moldavia.

Stefan had, as another issue of contention with Mathias, kept up his payment of tribute to the Ottomans, no doubt the wiser for having seen what had happened to Vlad when he had stopped paying. Indeed when Mehmed reacted to Stefan's conquest of the fortress at Chilia, by demanding that it be handed over to Wallachia, Stefan tried to pacify him by a voluntary increase of the tribute by 50%, followed by lavish gifts.

Even though that kept Mehmed at bay for a while, and he had other more immediate priorities, Stefan was well aware that the threat from Mehmed was far from gone, and instead of waiting for the Ottomans to strike he took a page from Vlad's book and went on the offensive himself.

Stefan's main concern was an Ottoman invasion coming through Wallachia, so he decided to get involved in Wallachian politics and install his own pliant ruler. To this end he was of course in good company as he was just continuing the external interference that had seen Wallachia in a position of turmoil for decades.

We have previously seen that there was never a shortage of possible contenders for the Wallachian throne, and Stefan's choice was Basarab Laiota, a son of the former Voivode, Dan II.

I have mentioned Dan II previously (in Chapter 2), as the Voivode who swapped thrones with his contemporary competitor (also called Radu) no less than four times in seven years in the 1420s. In a twist of fates, Basarab Laiota would come to match his father's record.

Basarab Laiota had been lingering in the background for years, but had never found support from a sufficient powerful party. With Stefan's designs on Wallachia that changed.

In 1470 Stefan entered Wallachia, where he got as far as Braila (which was routinely burned). In response Radu (with Ottoman backing) went into Moldavia the year following, but was beaten back.

A Tartar attempt to invade northern Moldavia (inspired by Genoese suspicion of Stefan's new power-politics) kept Stefan busy in 1472, but in 1473 he went to Wallachia again.

In November he defeated Radu at Rimnicu Sarat, and Laiota Basarab was put on the throne. An Ottoman attack across the Danube was beaten back, but followed only a month later by a more determined attack which saw Radu back on the Throne.

The following year Stefan came back and once again put Basarab Laiota on the throne. This time, however, Basarab Laiota must have figured out that his best chance of success in the long run was with the Ottomans, because he immediately turned on Stefan and declared his loyalty to Mehmed.

That of course was not the result Stefan had wanted, as his aim was to put a Voivode loyal to him on the throne of Wallachia, so he came again, this time ousting Basarab Laiota and putting yet another Voivode, Basarab Laiota's nephew, Basarab Cel Tanar on the throne. Basarab Laiota came back a few weeks later and beat Basarab Cel Tanar, only to once again be ousted by Stefan, ironically leaving Radu Cel Frumos back on the throne. Radu died in 1475 from natural causes, syphilis as it was, after which the Ottomans put Basarab Laiota back on the Wallachian throne.

If the period of internal stability, peace and prosperity experienced during Vlad's rule, despite his harsh reaction to transgressions, now started to look like "the good old days" to the common Wallachians, one can hardly blame them.

All in all little had been achieved except further stirring Mehmed's anger, a situation already aggravated by Stefan's refusal to pay tributes since 1473.

While Stefan was engaging himself in Wallachia, and Mathias was busy protecting his south-western border in Bosnia and Croatia, Mehmed had been busy in the east. The skirmishes in Wallachia had been left to smaller expedition forces and Mehmed's main army was engaged in the on-going battle with Uzun Hazan, his troublesome neighbor in eastern Anatolia. He had also been engaged in new hostilities with Venice, using his new fleet to battle it out for possession of a range of Venetian enclaves in and around the Mediterranean Sea.

By 1475 he had, however, had enough of Stefan, and he decided to execute his strategic objective of subjection of Moldavia, the missing piece in his increasingly strong steel-band around Hungary.

Mathias and Stefan, having been on hostile terms with each other for a decade, finally found each other in the common cause of defending against the forthcoming Ottoman invasion. Even though Mathias' contribution to Stefan's defending army only consisted of 1,800 troops, there was one important thing they also agreed on; the situation in Wallachia had to be sorted out.

Once again realising the Ottoman threat, the Hungarian Diet approved new funds for the raising of an army. Having learned from Mathias' previous use of funds designated for the army, but instead used to buy the Crown of St. Stephen, the money was specifically designated for fighting the Ottomans.

The army was raised and it was sent to Bosnia, a permanent theater of war, from where Ottoman raiders were consistently performing raids into Croatia, knocking on the door of Venice and the Italian mainland.

Even though Stefan would have probably preferred the army being deployed for his defense of Moldavia, the engagement in Bosnia meant the opening of a second front, and thus hopefully a division of Mehmed's attention and troops. Ahead of the new army rode none other than Vlad Dracula.

Stefan and Mathias had had a look at their options and had come up with the rather nostalgic choice of Vlad, echoing the sentiment of the common Wallachians.

Ignoring the former accusations of treason, which nobody really took seriously, Vlad was the only contestant who had shown capability to actually establish himself in Wallachia, and at the same time show clear loyalty to both Hungary and Moldavia.

After all, this was the same Vlad who had clearly supported the party that eventually put Mathias on the Hungarian throne and who had been the only one proactively assisting Stefan when he took the throne of Moldavia in 1457. He was thus acceptable to either party.

The Ottoman invasion of Moldavia turned into a disaster for Mehmed. Once again he was faced with an opponent fighting on their own ground and deploying guerilla tactics rather than open confrontation.

The Ottomans came in the winter, which in the opposite of the warm summer they had experienced in Wallachia in 1462, was unusually cold. The effect was the same though, as Stefan, like Vlad before him, burned the ground behind him, leaving the Ottomans with long and slow supply routes, which were easily attacked by Moldavian raiding parties.

Similar to the strategy deployed by Vlad's grand-father, Mircea Cel Batran, nearly 80 years before, Stefan picked his final battle ground carefully, choosing an area close to Vaslui, where forest, rivers and marshy fields prevented the Ottomans from deploying their army on a wide front, and thus taking advantage of their numeric superiority.

Further assisted by dense fog, the Moldavians bombarded the Ottomans with showers of arrows from positions hidden by the terrain and the fog. Rather than turning into an open battle, it turned into a rout, the Ottoman army fleeing the field, pursued by Moldavian cavalry.

The Ottoman army was severely decimated. Those that weren't killed were taken prisoners, and then impaled on the battlefield. And that atrocity was performed without Vlad's participation, as he was far away in Bosnia at the time.

Commander

You would have forgiven him if Vlad would have been caught pinching his arm to see if he was asleep or awake. Having endured thirteen years of de facto captivity, in which he was prevented from any active engagement in politics or warfare, rotting away in Pest and reduced to entertaining visiting dignitaries, here he was riding ahead of the Hungarian Army.

This was the same army in which he had put his hopes in 1462, and which had failed to materialise in his hour of need. Vlad was back, and with a vengeance.

Joined by Mathias himself, bringing further Hungarian troops in February of 1476, they conquered the Ottoman fortress in Sabac on the border region between Serbia and Bosnia, putting the captured Ottomans to death. Mathias then went back to Hungary, his cameo-appearance sufficient, and life in the field not compatible with his increasingly elegant lifestyle.

Vlad moved on, and took the mining-town of Srebrenica. Once again he used troops dressed as Ottomans to gain entry to the town itself. Having succeeded in his conquest, he impaled the Ottoman prisoners outside the walls. He then moved on to eradicate smaller Ottoman garrisons in Zwornik and Kuslat where he, according to the papal legate Gabriele Rangoni, 'tore the limbs off the Turkish prisoners and placed their parts on stakes'.

As a side note; Srebrenica was in 1941 the scene of a massacre of 1,000 Muslim civilians at the hand of Chetnik partisans and in 1995 the Serbian army killed 8,000 Muslim men and boys in and around Srebrenica. The Serbian army also killed hundreds of Muslim civilians (and destroyed the mosques) in Zvornik in 1992.

In the meantime, pressure was starting to build in Moldavia and Vlad hastened to help Stefan.

Mehmed had, due to bad health, not struck back at Moldavia immediately, but in the summer of 1476 he came back. This time he was better prepared, being supplied from a small naval force rather than overland, well knowing that Stefan would, once again, try to starve his army out.

Stefan's strategy had become predictable, so Mehmed managed to force him into battle at Rasboieni, a battle that was hard fought and in which the Ottoman army only prevailed due to Mehmed's personal presence. Stefan had to flee the field, though with very small losses and the timely arrival of Vlad and the Hungarian army, secured his safe retreat.

Mehmed's small supply fleet had in the meantime been hit by a storm, so he could not push his advantage, but had to retreat, having achieved little but a moral victory. Not surprisingly, Mehmed had been accompanied by a Wallachian contingent under the command of Basarab Laiota.

With the Ottoman army retreating, albeit unbeaten, the time was right to strike, so an expedition force consisting of a Hungarian army under the command of Stephen Barhory and Vlad, and the, mainly intact, Moldavian army marched on Wallachia from two different directions. The purpose was to get rid of the disloyal Basarab Laiota, and put Vlad Dracula back on the throne.

Last Stand

The invaders met Basarab Laiota's Wallachian army, reinforced by Ottoman troops, in a bloody battle at Rucar in the autumn of 1476. Though both sides suffered heavy losses it was Vlad's side that won the day, and by early November he was back in Targoviste, once again being elected Voivode. It would have been a brave Boyar that would have stood against him.

By the end of November he had taken Bucharest, his preferred town of government. The Hungarian and Moldavian troops now went back home, leaving him once again with a rather thin grip on power. Stefan however left a small contingent of 200 men to act as Vlad's household troops and bodyguard.

Contrary to his last ascension to the throne, where the incumbent Voivode was poorly supported by a weakened Ottoman Empire, Basarab Laiota was well supported and in December he came back with fresh Ottoman troops.

A small battle, more like a skirmish, broke out outside Bucharest, and during the battle Vlad Dracula died.

Exactly how he died is still a matter of debate. One version goes that he, dressed in Ottoman clothing, was mistakenly killed by one of his own. One version says he was killed by an assassin. One version has him executed by his Moldavian bodyguards.

Most agree that his head was cut off and brought to Mehmed, who had it exhibited in Istanbul, indicating that his body would have been in the possession of his adversaries and thus leaning towards the reasonable assumption that he was simply killed leading his troops from the front. Vlad lived by the sword, and he died by the sword.

Folklore has it that his (headless) body was brought to the monastery at Snagov, close to Bucharest, where to this day there is a memorial stone in front of the altar even though Vlad is not buried under it. This is not uncommon; indeed the use of a memorial stone without an actual body was a commonly used practice, but the fact that there is an empty hole under the stone still drive the vampire-hunters into a right frenzy.

The man Vlad was gone, but he left behind a legacy that would outlive him for centuries to come.

CHAPTER 7
LEGACY

Sir Jens

The Terror of His subjects

Franz Babinger was a very serious scholar and historian. His book *Mehmed der Eroberer und seine Zeit* (Mehmed the Conqueror and his Time) first published in 1953 is the absolute authority on all things Mehmed and the history of the Balkans in the latter half of the fifteenth century.

Babinger spoke several languages, including Persian, Hebrew, Romanian, Turkish and Arabic, so his access to original source-material was second to none.

Despite his otherwise meticulous sense of detail in his choice of sources, his description of Vlad is one based entirely on popular legacy. He writes the following:

'Ever since his accession to power in 1456, Vlad had been the terror of his subjects, his neighbors, and sometimes even of the Ottomans. His refined cruelty and bestial blood lust were unparalleled even in those barbarous times. By the thousands, those who had aroused his anger were impaled, cut to pieces, or burned alive. Long after his death his fame lived on even in Western Europe. As can be seen from the crude but impressive woodcuts to be found in incunabula printed in Augsburg, Bamberg, Nuremberg and Strasbourg.

His favorite sport was to dine with his court while a dense throng of freshly impaled Turks agonized nearby. He would order his henchmen to remove the skin from prisoner's feet, rub salt on the wounds, and bring in goats to lick it off. If an emissary from the sultan refused to bare his head when appearing before him, he would have three nails driven through the Turk's turban to make it all the more secure in accordance with tradition. One day he had all the beggars in the country invited to a banquet. After abundantly winning and dinning them, he had the hall set on fire and all perished in the flames. He would have the head of suckling babies impaled to their mothers; breasts. He forced children to eat pieces of their roasted mothers. He invented special devices for chopping people into hash, which would then be roasted or boiled. A monk whom he saw riding on an ass was impaled along with his mount. A priest who had preached that one should not lay hands on other people's possessions and who at table had eaten a piece of bread that Vlad had cut for himself was impaled on the spot. When one of his concubines thought herself pregnant but was not, he cut open her belly with his own hand. One hot summer day when Vlad was walking among the impaled, he was met by a worthy nobleman who asked him how he could bear the stench. Thereupon Vlad had the man impaled on the highest stake that could be found, in order to raise him above the stench.'

So when a man of Franz Babinger's reputation and pedigree as an academic in the twentieth century can form this opinion of Vlad Dracula, who in his own time was a crusader-hero and a popular icon of law and order, what had changed?

The explanation is multifaceted. It starts in Vlad's own time and continues through to our time even though there is a gap of nearly 400 years.

Vilified

If we go back to 1462, at the time where Vlad was expecting King Mathias to come to his assistance and drive the Ottomans out of Wallachia, and where instead he was arrested, this represented a real problem for Mathias.

The problem was that whereas Mathias was supposed to be leading the Christian crusade, and had taken the Pope's money to do just that, it was Vlad who had actually made war on Mehmed and had been praised by the Pope and Christian world in general for his initiative.

So when Mathias arrested Vlad, even with accusations of treason at hand, he expected a backlash from first and foremost the Pope and potentially also from other rulers, whom would be lackluster (to the extent they were not so already) to assist him in any future proposed campaigns against the Ottomans.

To kill Vlad was not an option, if it had been, he would have never left Brasov alive, so somehow Mathias had to justify his actions and swing popular opinion away from Vlad's achievements. He was in the end assisted by two very different people and a recent advancement in technology; a monk, a minnesinger (court-poet) and a printing press.

I have mentioned previously that Vlad was no friend of Catholic monks. He considered them a bunch of cheats and thieves, up to no good except for spying and spreading false religion. He had several run-ins with them in the early years of his reign and had even killed some as an example to the rest (whether with or without their mounts!).

He didn't kill them all though, and even though he would have seen them as a soft and weak breed, an irritant rather than a defined threat, he had overlooked the one weapon they possessed; they could write, and write they did.

Tucked away in monasteries, living in the shadows well away from Vlad's reach, they started to write about Vlad, whom they saw as an enemy of the (Catholic) Church and thus of Christ himself.

That exaggeration improves the understanding was a well known fact even then, indeed fifteenth century chronicles consistently overstate numbers in order to impress, so rather than just write down the facts (which would have probably not raised that many eyebrows in a rather brutal world) they exaggerated, and when exaggeration wasn't enough, they just made it up, often based on real-life events that just didn't actually have anything to do with Vlad.

Meticulous as they were, monks returning or visiting from the Saxon cities of Transylvania and from Wallachia itself brought tales of horror (which they may or may not have actually witnessed) and they were improved upon and written down. No less than thirty-two short, but gruesome, tales would eventually be kept in the library at the monastery of St. Gall in Switzerland. That in itself would have probably not really hurt Vlad's reputation much as monastic writings rarely went much further than a rather narrow audience.

As relatively harmless as these tales were, tucked away outside the reach of the general public, they would start to make a direct impact on Vlad's reputation through what was probably a chance encounter between a monk called Brother Jacob and a minnesinger called Michel Beheim.

Beheim was an established minnesinger, who in the years around 1460 was in the employment of the Holy Roman Emperor Frederich III. As was the role of minnesingers he wrote and performed poetry, mostly in the form of songs, dealing with Christian virtues, love or recent events.

Whether it was a chance encounter, or whether he was perhaps talking to Brother Jacob to gather news on recent events, Brother Jacob had a story to tell, namely his own, further improved, summary of the monastic stories about Vlad Dracula.

To Beheim that was just too good a story to ignore, so he sat down and composed a poem titled *Von ainem wutrich der heis Trakle waida von der Walachei* (The Story of a Bloodthirsty Madman Called Dracula of Wallachia) that he also put to music. He would have improved the story further, or as in the words of Elizabeth Miller in her article *Beheim and the Dracula Connection*:

'*The Dracula poem shares many of the characteristics of Beheim's other works, specifically a tendency to exaggerate numbers for political purposes, to invent conversations of which there is no record, even to manufacture incidents. For Beheim, historical accuracy was less important than adherence to the central principle that history is a vehicle shaped at will and intended to promote a particular political point of view.*'

The finished works was first performed to Emperor Frederich sometime in the winter of 1463, more or less exactly a year after Vlad's arrest. Frederich is said to have absolutely loved it, and it was written down and even translated into Latin.

Around the time Vlad took the throne of Wallachia for the second time, a German by the name of Johann Gutenberg had just starting mass-producing books using a new and revolutionary technique; printing.

Gutenberg could from his workshop in Mainz produce multiple copies of books based on a single original set of letters arranged in frames. He was notoriously poor and in constant debt, but had found a patron in the Church, so he made bibles.

Gutenberg's invention soon spread, particularly in Germany, where all bigger cities soon had their own printing press. First they produced mainly religious material, but as much as that was a great moral thing to do, there wasn't that much money in it (it is worth remembering that this is before the Reformation, so religious literature was not aimed at the population in general) .

The fifteenth century was no different from our own time; if you wanted to sell a story then sex, violence and scandal would give you a significantly broader audience than religious pamphlets, and the story of Vlad Dracula had it all.

Through the new printing press in Vienna the story of Vlad Dracula, grossly distorted and exaggerated as it was, became one of the first mass produced non-religious books.

Exactly how, or to whom, the book was distributed is unknown, but Mathias would have ensured that those of importance, one can assume this included the Pope, who had not had the opportunity to hear Michel Beheim's original song would now read the book.

There is speculation that Mathias proactively sponsored the printing of the book, and in particular the version in Latin, but as possible as that is, it is unsubstantiated.

When the book started to circulate, sometime around 1464, Vlad's reputation thus started to go from famous to infamous, and though some would have heard of him already, many would hear of him now.

Eleven years later, when King Mathias needed Vlad to once again clean up the mess that Wallachia had become,

Mathias seems to have gladly ignored both the former charges of treason and the attempts at character assassination. Those served a purpose at the time, but reality soon overrode their original intentions.

If it had stayed like that, then Vlad Dracula would probably have been yet another anonymous Wallachian Voivode, forgotten by time but not necessarily by his people, his life reflected in folklore and a dusty old book.

But in the 1480s, ten years or so after the death of Vlad Dracula and twenty years since the original publishing of Beheim's poem, printing presses had spread and the need for new material was increasing with a new, literate, audience quickly building throughout Europe.

The story of Vlad was dusted off, improved, expanded and woodcuts were made to accompany the story. Several new editions were printed, culminating around the year 1500, from where the woodcuts referred to by Franz Babinger also belong. Vlad was still selling twenty-five years or so after his death, but then the novelty and newsworthiness gradually faded away.

Entering the sixteenth century, new and more recent events overtook old tales about a long dead ruler of a small place called Wallachia.

It would take nearly 400 years before someone rediscovered Dracula in a way that would make him immortal but yet at the same time move his legacy even further away from the man he really was.

Immortal

Bram Stoker was an Irish civil servant with a love of writing and theater. He specifically wrote horror novels, and in 1897 he published the book 'Dracula'.

The book was originally, and up until a few weeks before its publication, called 'The Un-dead" and the main character was called 'Count Wampyr'.

Stoker had done extensive research of, in particular European, tales of vampires and other creatures of the night. Somewhere along the line, and late in the process, he came across Dracula and Transylvania.

There is no evidence that Bram Stoker ever had access to, or indeed any knowledge of, any of the tales about Vlad Dracula, neither the folklore, nor the tales hidden away in monasteries or indeed any of the printed matters of the late fifteenth century.

His sole inspiration seems to have been a book, published in 1820, by British diplomat William Wilkinson named *An Account of the Principalities of Wallachia and Moldavia: With Various Political Observations Relating to Them* in which the name Dracula is used for both Vlad Dracul and Vlad Dracula and in which a footnote mentions that:

'Dracula in the Wallachian language means Devil. The Wallachians were, at that time, as they are at present, used to give this as a surname to any person who rendered himself conspicuous either by courage, cruel actions, or cunning'

The mention of Dracula (both of them) is short and mainly focused on the content of the agreement between Vlad and Mehmed from 1460, but that was all Stoker needed.

With an eye for catchy names he decided to change his manuscript to incorporate the name Dracula and the location of Transylvania.

Stoker was never in Transylvania, but he owned a map, so with Transylvania came a couple of other geographical references, Klausenburg (modern day Cluj-Napoca and the birth town of King Mathias), Bistrita and, not least, the Borgo Pass.

Though Vlad did raid Bistrita in 1457, the reference made by Stoker is coincidental, you basically get there by running a finger east from Budapest (passing through Klausenburg/Cluj-Napoca on the way). And if you are looking for scenic setting for a castle, the Borgo Pass, close to Bistrita, is perfect.

It is not a lot to go on really, a name and a location, but it was all that was needed and 400 years after his death Vlad Dracula truly became immortal.

Fact of the matter is that if Bram Stoker had not decided to use the name Dracula, and place him in Transylvania, then I would not be writing this book and even if I did, you probably wouldn't be reading it.

Heroes

Up until, and including, the First World War, the losing countries of major conflicts were traditionally carved up according to the will of the winners and even though the ruler would rarely survive, no individuals would normally be held to account for their deeds during the conflict itself.

The Nuremberg Trials in 1945/1946 however set new precedence for how we in the twentieth, leading into the twenty-first, century look at war, both in terms of warfare itself and its consequences on civilians.

For the first time did the world community, or rather the winners of the Second World War, and France, on behalf of the world community, proactively prosecute those perceived to be responsible for serious war crimes and/or crimes against humanity.

Other trials have followed, e.g. the trial of Slobodan Milosevic in 2001 and the trial of Sadam Hussein in 2006.

Vlad Dracula is the main character of this book, it is his story we follow, but around him three characters form up in strong supporting roles; Mehmed, Mathias and Stefan.

From a modern view, all of these four were criminals, guilty of war crimes and crimes against humanity. All four killed prisoners and civilians alike, and all four used torture on captured enemies to gather intelligence. If any of them would be put on trial today they would be condemned and executed.

That, however, is retrofitting our contemporary standards onto a time where reality was very different and the standards, indeed the expectations, upon which a ruler or military commander were judged was considerably different.

Each of these four men is different, but then again they are very alike and one thing they have in common is that to their people they are all heroes.

Vlad's role as a hero is already established. Independently from the written tales, leading us from fifteenth century monasteries to Bram Stoker, Romanian folklore is clear in it verdict; Vlad is a man of the people, a bringer of law and order, a protector of the weak and a champion of Christianity.

Mehmed's moniker is 'Fatih', the conqueror. He finally gave the Ottomans the long treasured prize of Constantinople and showed great statesmanship in his very deliberate lenient treatment of religious and cultural minorities. If you go to modern day Turkey, the face you will see from pictures and posters the most is that of Ataturk the father of the modern Turkish Republic. The face you will see the second-most is that of Fatih Sultan Mehmed. He is a hero, if not an outright icon, of Ottoman greatness and supremacy.

Mathias is a hero of Hungary to this day, not because he really achieved much (I have mentioned earlier that he never actually fought a full-scale battle with the Ottomans), but because he came from the people rather than some external royal bloodline. He symbolises a strong Hungary independent from foreign influence and his picture, and statues, can be seen throughout Hungary and Transylvania.

Stefan was given the moniker "Cel Mare" (The Great). He is seen as someone who stood up against all enemies (including Hungary), protected a strong Moldavia and who proactively fought the enemies of Christianity. On 20 June 1992 the Synodic Council of the Romanian Orthodox Church canonised Stefan under the name 'Saint Voivode Stephen the Great'. Stefan is not just a hero he is, officially, a saint.

On the notion that government exists to serve the people and we thus accept that it is the people whom these four rulers served who should decide on their legacy, then the verdicts are clear, despite how we would look at them today.

As a closing note on the subject, during my research for this book I came upon one more interesting link between Vlad and Mathias; they are both "sleeping kings" a term used to cover the various rulers who, across time and geography, have been connected to the similar tale of "the king in the mountain" myth, in which there is a mountain (or, in lieu of a mountain, a dungeon) in which a powerful and capable ruler of past is sleeping, and from where he will awake and once more come to the rescue of his people in their hour of need. *'Rise once more, o Tepeş'*.

CHAPTER 8
MEET DRACULA

Sir Jens

Where is Dracula?

You may recall that in the Foreword of this book I explain how my personal search for Vlad started with the question 'Where is Dracula?'

I was in Transylvania, but Dracula seemed to be missing. We now know that is because the historic Vlad Dracula was not actually from Transylvania, even though he, in some more modern aspects, has become a pan-Romanian national hero.

But Vlad's apparent lack of presence in Transylvania does not mean he can't be found, even though you will need to go a bit further than Transylvania itself.

If you want to find Vlad, you basically have two options available. One option is to go vampire-hunting and the other is to follow the historic trail.

I will deal with both following.

The Retro-fitted Vampire

As you, the reader, will now be aware, Dracula's status as a vampire is not historical, but rather a nineteenth century invention, linking a catchy name to an already finished work of horror-fiction.

With that in mind, everything linking Vlad Dracula to anything vampire is a retro-fit.

There are plenty of books, and web-sites, linking Vlad Dracula to vampirism, and it is not my mission to do likewise, rather on the contrary. Instead I will briefly cover the worst contemporary tourist traps so, should you decide to take one of the commonly offered packaged "Dracula Tours", then you will at least understand what you are looking at.

I will cover the real "Dracula's Castle" in some detail following, so let us get the tourist traps out of the way first.

There is no castle in the Borgo Pass. Not Dracula's castle, not any other castle. There is a hotel, built in the 1970s, aptly called "Castel Dracula" (Dracula's Castle). Romanian countryside hotels are notoriously sub-standard, both in terms of accommodation, service and food, and this one is no exception. It does have a small Dracula exhibit, where a man dressed up as a vampire jumps out to scare the children, and outside there are a few souvenir sellers. If this is your scene, knock yourself out, but don't think that you have been anywhere near the historic Vlad Dracula.

There is a castle in Bran, south of Brasov. It is however (and despite what you read on the Internet and in glossy brochures touting tours) not Dracula's Castle. It is a former medieval border post, controlling the border between Transylvania and Wallachia. It did belong to Wallachia in the fifteenth century and it would probably have been used by Vlad Dracula as a stop-over on a couple of occasions when he was on his way to Brasov. But that is it.

Bran castle belongs (once again) to the Romanian Royal Family and it was re-built in faux gothic style in the early twentieth century. It is a lovely little castle, with a very charming central courtyard, and a rather boring collection of un-original furniture. There is no Dracula exhibition in the castle, indeed Dracula is not mentioned at all, which is because it is not Dracula's castle.

If you want to buy Dracula souvenirs, the kind of stuff I originally thought I would find on every street-corner in Transylvania, then the market-area at the bottom of Bran Castle is packed with such trinkets of deceit. If you don't, then leave Bran Castle to the busloads of tourists and go do something real.

The monastery in Snagov, or rather on an island on Snagov Lake, is the reputed burial place of Vlad Dracula. Historically Vlad is known to have given money to Snagov Monastery, as well as other monasteries, and folklore has it that his body was brought there after he was killed in battle in 1476. There is no historical evidence to back that up. There is a stone in the floor in front of the altar which, despite being plain and un-inscribed, is said to mark the grave of Vlad. When it was removed in the 1930s an empty hole was found under it (which makes a nice retro-fit should you be the vampire-kind). Today there is even a cheap souvenir-class picture of Vlad (probably bought at Bran Castle) placed on the stone to make sure you find what you are looking for. There are lots of nice monasteries in Romania, Snagov is one of them, but not the easiest to get to. If you feel you need to go, it is no doubt an experience, but beware that you have not found the historic Vlad Dracula.

Contrary to any of the places mentioned above, a place well worth visiting is Hunyadi Castle in Hunedoara. It has no direct link to Vlad Dracula, even though you may be fed a story of how Vlad slaved away a decade of captivity there in order to build up some excitement. It is however the family castle of the Hunyadi family, and thus of both Janos and Mathias Hunyadi, and it is likely that it was here that Vlad and Janos got reconciled sometime in early 1452. The castle is big and imposing and in a rather good condition despite centuries of neglect. If you have the opportunity to go, do so, but do it because of the castle itself, not because you will find Dracula.

Dracula's Castle

So why is it that you will readily be sold visits to castles that are not really Dracula's castle?

The answer is that there is no real Dracula's castle to take you to, or at least not in the real sense of Dracula's castle.

When we use the term Dracula's castle we kind of imply that it is somewhere Dracula actually lived, assumingly with his family, and which was the centre of his existence. And therein lays the problem. Vlad Dracula didn't live in a castle.

Vlad, as ruler of Wallachia, lived in the royal compound in Targoviste, which isn't a castle. The main building in the Targoviste compound is a palace-building which would have contained both residential quarters and administrative offices. There is also a church, a watch-tower (called the Chindia Tower and allegedly built during Vlad's reign) and the remnants of various outbuildings. The compound is built on flat ground with a surrounding wall strong enough to repel a peasant uprising, but no match for a determined army.

Today the palace is a fantastic ruin, that is if you are the type of person who doesn't mind going around on your own to observe the past without the need of a bus, a tour guide, a support group and an obligatory visit to a nearby crafts-centre. The restored Chindia Tower contains an exhibition of letters from the historic Vlad Dracula, or at least it did when I was there. Also, when I went, the person selling (cheap) tickets and a small selection of souvenirs from a hut by the entrance was (temporarily) missing, so I paid my admission on exit. This is Romanian tourism at its absolute best and a must go if you want to meet Vlad Dracula.

As a twist of irony, Targoviste also has a small museum with the first printing press in Romania, though by the time (1521) that was first used to print Romanian, Vlad was long gone and nearly forgotten.

If the palace in Targoviste just doesn't do it for you in terms of a castle, then don't despair, there is a castle!

The castle is in Poienari, and in terms of castles it is as close to Dracula's castle as you will get. This is the very castle that Vlad modernized, allegedly by means of boyars turned slave laborers, and in which he sought refuge in 1462 after having given up active resistance against the invading Ottomans (and from which his wife would have thrown herself in the river).

A good part of the castle was destroyed by a landslide in 1888 but some repair-work has been done and the castle still stands.

It is located high up on a steep precipice of rock, dominating the surrounding area, and the narrow valley beneath it, just the way a castle should. It is authentic, it is historic, it just isn't where Vlad Dracula lived, except for the short period of time during his refuge in 1462.

Like Bran castle, Poienari was basically a border-post and customs-station on the border between Wallachia and Transylvania. It was not a big "battle castle" full of gallant knights, grim mercenaries and white-skinned ladies.

That said it is a superb place to visit, but it is for the fit. Today there are stairs winding up through the forest, no less than 1480 of them, and at the top you get to buy your ticket, so don't forget your change in the car!

The view from the castle is fantastic, and you will know that you share something with Vlad.

At the bottom there is a small stall selling water and a very small selection of bric-a-brac. There is also now a new motel, which is not bad at all (we took refuge for a night having been caught by a thunderstorm).

Poienari is a must if you are looking for Dracula. It is the real deal, but given its location high up and far away from any major towns, it is easy to understand why Bran castle is touted as Dracula's castle as it is significantly easier to get to for tourists more concerned about what is for lunch than whether anything they are told is indeed true.

Back to the Beginning

We can suitably end the story where it began, namely in Sighisoara, which is in Transylvania.

Sighisoara has a citadel, a fortified hilltop compound that in times of trouble would have served as safe-haven for the locals and their livestock.

The Saxon walls here are significantly more formidable than those surrounding the royal compound in Targoviste, and there are several imposing towers and bastions still standing.

The compound is unique not only in its originality and state of preservation, but also from the fact that the small houses, dating back hundreds of years, are still lived in even though fires have destroyed most houses from the fifteenth century.

Just off the main square stands the three-storey house where Vlad Dracula was born.

You would expect some signposts and a ticket-booth, but no. There s a small plaque on the wall, stating the fact that this is the house where Vlad Dracula was born in 1431, and the building itself contains a half-decent restaurant kept in medieval style with wood-paneled walls.

The citadel also contains a big clock-tower, which can be visited, and a small arms museum, but really the main attraction is to just walk around, not least up to the top of the hill where the school is and where there is a beautiful peaceful German cemetery.

Together with Poienari, Sighisoara is a must do. Do yourself a favor and stay for a night, it looks fantastic at night-time. There are plenty of hotels inside the citadel itself (no; you cannot stay in Dracula's house).

And that is really it. I hope you can now answer the question "Where is Dracula?" should it come up in casual conversation.

###

Sir Jens

NOTES

First of all, I hoped you enjoyed the book. It was a challenge to write, so hopefully it was easy to read.

If you are further interested in the subject, then please join me and other readers in my "Authors' Corner" at www.SirJens.com where I have a section with Recommended Reading as well as my pictures of some of the places that are mentioned in this book.

Regarding the book itself, there are a few notes worth mentioning.

Most important is to repeat that a lot of details regarding Vlad Dracula are sketchy. There are some surviving letters, and some first-hand accounts, but over and above that there is a lot of noise, some created in the late 1400s, some much more recent when people have been trying to retrofit a specific view on Vlad Dracula (vampire or otherwise) onto history. I have tried to be specific as to what is real and what is speculation and I hope I have succeeded.

You may have noted that I have consistently used the term "Ottomans" instead of "Turks". That is very much on purpose as the Ottomans did not label themselves as being Turks. The word "Turk" was invented by Latin (Western European) people as a not overly polite term and only became adopted into what we now consider Turkish culture when it was used to name the new Turkish Republic in 1923.

The same could be said about what I have called "Byzantines", in that they called themselves "Romans", but that just gets too confusing and I have only retained the name "Rumelia" for the European part of modern day Turkey.

ABOUT THE AUTHOR

I was an Army Officer when I was young, but I have spent twenty years as a leader in various software and telecoms organisations, including some blue-chip companies. Though Danish I have spent two decades outside my native country, living and working on three different continents. I have now retired from working-life and concentrate on pursuing my life-long hobby as an amateur-historian.

Made in the USA
Lexington, KY
12 February 2014